The Telematics Revolution: Driving Connectivity and Insights

Exploring the intersection of technology and connectivity in a rapidly evolving world

Anand Kumar Vedantham

About The Author

Anand Kumar Vedantham is a technology leader and architect with over 17 years of expertise in cloud computing, telematics, and realtime data integration. Specializing in Microsoft Azure and IoT solutions, he has led transformative projects in the automotive and agriculture industries. A thought leader in connected technologies and IoT solutions, Anand Kumar is deeply passionate about innovation, knowledge sharing, and shaping the future of smart systems.

Acknowledgments

This book would not have been possible without the incredible support and encouragement of the people around me.

I am deeply grateful to my parents, **Venkat** and **Vasumati**, for their endless love, support, and encouragement throughout my journey.

To my wonderful wife, **Swapna**, your unwavering love, patience, and belief in me have been my anchor. Thank you for always standing by my side and inspiring me every day.

To my amazing daughter, **Teekshika,** your curiosity and boundless energy remind me why I pursue knowledge and creativity. You are my greatest source of joy and motivation.

To my esteemed Managers & Colleagues, **Srinivas Mallela, Bartłomiej Budz, Phanikumar Kanumilli, Heera Nair, Sachin Chaudhari, and Suresh Pabba**, your expertise, collaboration, and support have been instrumental in shaping the ideas and research behind this book. Working alongside you has been both an honor and a privilege.

Finally, to all those who have shared their knowledge and passion for technology, connectivity, and innovation, thank you for being a part of the foundation on which this book is built.

This book is a testament to the power of support, inspiration, and community.

Dedication

To the technology community, the innovators, the dreamers, the problem-solvers.

Your relentless pursuit of progress, your passion for connectivity, and your vision for a better tomorrow inspire the world to dream bigger and achieve more.

This book is for you, the architects of the connected future.

Contents

Introduction

In an era defined by rapid technological innovation, telematics has emerged as a cornerstone of connectivity, data-driven insights, and transformative change. This book, *The Future of Telematics: Connecting Vehicles, Data, and Insights*, delves into the evolving role of telematics and its profound influence on industries, communities, and our daily lives.

Telematics is no longer just about vehicles; it is a dynamic technology that integrates real-time data, connectivity, and advanced analytics to enhance decision-making, improve safety, and foster efficiency. From autonomous vehicles and smart transportation systems to predictive analytics in logistics, telematics represents a critical shift toward a more intelligent and interconnected world.

This book is crafted to:

1. **Simplify Complexity:** Breaking down the advanced concepts of telematics into actionable insights.

2. **Showcase Real-World Impact:** Exploring how telematics is being applied across sectors such as automotive, logistics, urban planning, and more.

3. **Highlight Future Possibilities:** Examining emerging trends, challenges, and opportunities for innovation in this rapidly evolving field.

Whether you're a technologist, a business leader, or a curious reader, *The Future of Telematics* will provide a comprehensive exploration of how this technology is reshaping industries and driving us toward a smarter, more connected future.

As we embark on this exploration, let us reflect on the collaborative spirit of the global technology community, whose vision and innovation continue to push boundaries and redefine possibilities.

Together, we are shaping a future where vehicles, data, and insights converge to empower and inspire.

Welcome to *The Future of Telematics*.

Chapter 1
Introduction to Telematics

Introduction

Imagine a world where vehicles communicate with each other, traffic flows seamlessly, and businesses optimize operations in real time. Welcome to the realm of telematics—a fusion of telecommunications and informatics that transforms how we connect, communicate, and make decisions.

This chapter introduces telematics, exploring its definition, history, components, and significance in our modern, data-driven world. It also sheds light on how telematics has evolved from simple vehicle tracking to shaping connected ecosystems and paving the way for future innovations.

What is Telematics?

Telematics combines telecommunications and informatics, enabling the seamless transmission of data over vast networks. At its core, telematics systems integrate hardware, software, and data analytics to gather, process, and share real-time information.

Initially designed for basic vehicle tracking, telematics now powers connected vehicles, fleet management systems, and smart cities. By bridging data and connectivity, it transforms industries and enhances daily life.

Example: A telematics device in a vehicle not only tracks its location but also monitors fuel efficiency, alerts drivers to maintenance needs, and provides real-time navigation.

A Brief History of Telematics

Telematics has a fascinating history, evolving alongside advancements in technology:

1. **1960s-1970s: Early Foundations**

   o Satellite communication systems emerged, leading to the launch of the first GPS satellite in 1978.

   o Military applications dominated, enabling precise navigation and tracking.

2. **1980s: Technology Emergence**

   o GPS became available for civilian use (1983), sparking the development of fleet management systems.

   o Cellular networks enabled basic data transmission, and the term "telematics" was coined.

3. **1990s: Commercial Growth**

   o GPS became fully operational, and services like OnStar revolutionized vehicle diagnostics and emergency response.

   o The introduction of OBD-II standards set the stage for modern vehicle data collection.

4. **2000s: Integration Era**

   o Real-time traffic updates, usage-based insurance, and IoT integration became mainstream.

   o 3G networks supported faster data transmission.

5. **2010s: The Connected Revolution**

   o 4G LTE enabled seamless connectivity between vehicles and smartphones.

   o Advanced driver assistance systems (ADAS) and IoT-powered telematics gained prominence.

6. **2020s and Beyond: Advanced Applications**

   o 5G networks, AI, and machine learning power autonomous vehicles and V2X (vehicle-to-everything) communication.

   o Cybersecurity and blockchain technologies enhance data integrity and system security.

From Vehicle Tracking to Connected Ecosystems

Telematics has transformed from simple vehicle tracking to creating connected ecosystems where vehicles, infrastructure, and devices communicate seamlessly.

- **Fleet Management**: Businesses optimize routes, monitor driver behavior, and reduce fuel costs.

- **Smart Cities**: Traffic signals, public transportation, and parking systems integrate with telematics for real-time optimization.

- **Autonomous Vehicles**: Advanced telematics systems support self-driving cars by enabling vehicle-to-vehicle (V2V) and vehicle-to-infrastructure (V2I) communication.

Example: In a smart city, telematics-enabled vehicles can reroute themselves during heavy traffic, reducing congestion and emissions.

Core Components of Telematics

Telematics systems consist of four key components that work together seamlessly:

1. **Hardware**: Sensors, GPS modules, and onboard diagnostics (OBD) devices capture real-time data.

2. **Connectivity**: Wireless technologies like 4G/5G, Wi-Fi, and Bluetooth transmit data across networks.

3. **Software Platforms**: Cloud-based systems process, analyze, and store data, providing actionable insights via user-friendly dashboards.

4. **Data Analytics**: Algorithms turn raw data into valuable insights, enabling predictive maintenance, route optimization, and more.

Why Telematics Matters

Telematics is a game-changer across industries, delivering benefits that include:

- **Efficiency**: Optimizes routes, reduces fuel consumption, and minimizes operational downtime.

- **Safety**: Monitors driving behavior, detects risks, and alerts emergency services during accidents.

- **Cost Savings**: Streamlines processes, cutting operational expenses.

- **Data-Driven Insights**: Predictive analytics enable proactive decision-making, improving outcomes across industries.

Real-World Impact: A logistics company saved 20% on fuel costs by adopting telematics for route optimization and driver monitoring.

Telematics Today and Tomorrow

Today, telematics drives transformative technologies like smart cities, autonomous vehicles, and predictive analytics. Looking ahead, its potential is limitless with the integration of:

- **5G Connectivity**: Enables ultra-fast data exchange for real-time applications.

- **AI and Machine Learning**: Enhances predictive analytics and personalization.

- **Blockchain**: Provides secure and transparent data sharing.

- **V2X Communication**: Facilitates seamless interaction between vehicles and infrastructure.

The future of telematics lies in creating a fully connected world, revolutionizing transportation, logistics, and beyond.

Key Takeaways

- Telematics combines telecommunications and informatics, enabling real-time data exchange.

- It has evolved from basic GPS tracking to driving connected ecosystems and autonomous technologies.

- Its benefits span efficiency, safety, and cost savings, with applications across industries.

- Emerging technologies like 5G and AI will shape the next chapter in telematics.

Chapter 2
The Building Blocks of Telematics

Introduction

Telematics systems are powered by a sophisticated interplay of technologies, each serving a critical role in capturing, processing, and transmitting data. From sensors in vehicles to real-time analytics in the cloud, these building blocks enable telematics to transform industries and drive innovation.

Consider this: Telematics systems are projected to save logistics companies billions of dollars annually by 2030 through route optimization, fuel efficiency, and predictive maintenance (Frost & Sullivan, 2023). This chapter explores the core components of telematics, the role of IoT, emerging technologies, and the challenges and opportunities they present.

Core Components of Telematics Systems

Telematics systems rely on four foundational components that work together to deliver functionality and insights:

1. **Hardware**

    o **Sensors**: Devices that capture environmental and vehicular data, such as speed, location, and temperature.

    o **On-Board Diagnostics (OBD-II)**: Interfaces that provide real-time diagnostics and vehicle performance data (GPS.gov, 2023).

GPS Modules: Essential for location tracking and navigation, with brands like u-blox leading the market (International Transport Forum, 2022).

Example: A telematics-enabled truck uses OBD-II to monitor engine health, preventing costly breakdowns.

2. **Connectivity**

   o **Cellular Networks (4G/5G)**: Ensure real-time data transmission over long distances.

     o **Bluetooth and Wi-Fi**: Enable short-range communication between devices.

     o **Satellite Communication**: Provides connectivity in remote or hard-to-reach areas.

Example: 5G networks reduce latency for real-time applications, enabling autonomous vehicle responses in milliseconds (Allied Market Research, 2023).

3. **Software Platforms**

     o Cloud platforms like AWS IoT Core and Azure IoT process and store vast amounts of telematics data, converting it into actionable insights (International Data Corporation, 2022).

     o User-friendly dashboards display analytics for fleet managers and drivers.

4. **Data Analytics**

     o Algorithms analyze raw data to predict vehicle failures, optimize routes, and identify cost-saving opportunities.

- o AI and machine learning enable predictive and prescriptive insights (McKinsey & Company, 2021).

The Role of IoT in Telematics

The Internet of Things (IoT) connects vehicles, devices, and infrastructure, amplifying telematics' capabilities:

- **V2X Communication**:
  - o Vehicle-to-Vehicle (V2V): Cars share data like speed and proximity to avoid collisions.
  - o Vehicle-to-Infrastructure (V2I): Interacts with traffic signals and road systems for efficient navigation.

Example: Smart traffic lights use IoT and telematics to dynamically adjust signal timing based on traffic flow (Frost & Sullivan, 2023).

- **Real-World Applications**:
  - o Fleet operators monitor fuel usage and driver behavior using IoT-enabled sensors.
  - o Smart cities reduce congestion with IoT-driven traffic management systems.

Emerging Technologies Enhancing Telematics

1. **5G Networks**
   - o Enable ultra-fast, reliable data exchange for real-time applications like autonomous driving.

   - o Reduce latency, critical for split-second decisionmaking in connected vehicles (Allied Market Research, 2023).

2. **Edge Computing**
   - Processes data closer to its source, reducing dependency on centralized systems and enabling faster responses.
   - **Example**: An autonomous vehicle uses edge computing to process sensor data and avoid obstacles instantly.
3. **Blockchain**
   - Ensures secure, tamper-proof data sharing among stakeholders.
   - **Example**: Fleet managers track vehicle maintenance and fuel records on a blockchain for transparency (McKinsey & Company, 2021).
4. **AI and Machine Learning**
   - Enhance telematics systems by providing predictive insights, such as identifying potential mechanical failures before they occur.
   - AI personalizes user experiences, such as tailoring insurance premiums based on driving behavior.

Challenges in Building Telematics Systems

Despite its potential, telematics faces several hurdles:

1. **Infrastructure Costs**

   - High initial investments in hardware, software, and connectivity.

   - Mitigation: Phased implementations and government subsidies can offset costs (Frost & Sullivan, 2023).

2. **Data Security Concerns**

   - Cyber threats pose risks to sensitive data.

- o Mitigation: Encrypt data during transmission and conduct regular security audits (McKinsey & Company, 2021).

3. **Interoperability**

- o Integrating telematics with legacy systems can be complex.

- o Mitigation: Adopt standardized protocols and APIs to improve compatibility.

Real-World Case Study

Fleet Management Optimization:

A global logistics company implemented telematics by integrating GPS tracking, IoT sensors, and AI-powered analytics.

- **Results:**
  - o **Reduced fuel consumption by 20%.**
  - o **o Improved delivery times by 30%.**
  - o **Enhanced safety through proactive maintenance alerts (Frost & Sullivan, 2023).**

Key Takeaways

- Telematics systems rely on hardware, connectivity, software, and data analytics to deliver seamless functionality (International Data Corporation, 2022).
- IoT and emerging technologies like 5G and blockchain are revolutionizing telematics applications.
- Addressing challenges such as infrastructure costs and security risks will be key to widespread adoption.

- Real-world applications like fleet management showcase telematics' transformative potential.

Chapter 3
Applications of Telematics in Transportation

Introduction

Telematics has emerged as a cornerstone of the transportation industry, transforming operations with its ability to connect vehicles, infrastructure, and data systems in real time. By integrating advanced analytics, IoT, and connectivity, telematics enhances efficiency, safety, and sustainability.

Consider this: Companies that adopt telematics in their fleet operations report a 20% reduction in fuel consumption and a 30% improvement in delivery times (Frost & Sullivan, 2023). This chapter explores the diverse applications of telematics in transportation, focusing on smart vehicles, fleet management, road safety, and public transit.

1. Smart Vehicles and Driver Assistance Systems

Telematics powers smart vehicles with technologies that improve safety and user experience:

1. **Predictive Maintenance**:

    o   Telematics monitors critical vehicle parameters, such as engine health and tire pressure, alerting drivers to potential issues before they escalate.

    Example: BMW uses telematics to notify drivers of maintenance needs via connected apps (McKinsey & Company, 2021).

2. **Driver Assistance Systems**:

  - o Advanced Driver Assistance Systems (ADAS) rely on telematics for lane-keeping, adaptive cruise control, and collision avoidance.

  - o **Example**: Tesla's autopilot uses real-time telematics data to adjust speed, monitor lane changes, and prevent collisions (Allied Market Research, 2023).

3. **Infotainment and Connectivity**:

  - o Drivers benefit from seamless integration with navigation, media, and communication systems, reducing distractions.

4. **Electric Vehicles (EVs)**:

  - o Telematics enables real-time battery health monitoring, route optimization with charging stations, and energy grid integration.

  - o **Example**: Rivian EVs leverage telematics to plan routes based on charging station availability (Frost & Sullivan, 2023).

2. Fleet Management and Logistics Optimization

Telematics revolutionizes fleet operations by optimizing routes, enhancing safety, and improving cost-efficiency:

1. **Route Optimization**:

  - o GPS and real-time traffic data help identify the shortest and least congested routes.

  - o **Example**: UPS reduced miles driven by 10 million annually using telematics for route planning (International Transport Forum, 2022).

2. **Driver Behavior Monitoring**:

   o   Metrics such as harsh braking, speeding, and idling are analyzed to improve driver safety and fuel efficiency.

   o   **Example**: A logistics firm reduced accidents by 25% after implementing driver behavior tracking systems (McKinsey & Company, 2021).

3. **Fuel Efficiency**:

   o   Telematics tracks consumption patterns, helping companies cut costs and reduce emissions.

   o   **Case Study**: A delivery company saved 15% annually on fuel costs through telematics-based optimization (Frost & Sullivan, 2023).

4. **Asset Tracking**:

   o   Real-time tracking ensures the security and integrity of transported goods, monitoring conditions such as temperature for perishable items.

5. **Predictive Maintenance**:

   o   Telematics minimizes downtime by detecting and addressing vehicle issues before they disrupt operations.

3. Enhancing Road Safety with Telematics

Safety remains a top priority in transportation, and telematics contributes significantly:

1. **Crash Detection and Emergency Response**:

   o   Telematics systems send automatic crash notifications to emergency services, improving response times.

- o **Example**: GM's OnStar system alerts first responders with precise crash locations (Allied Market Research, 2023).

2. **Driver Fatigue Monitoring**:

- o Sensors detect signs of fatigue, such as erratic steering or prolonged eye closure, prompting drivers to take breaks.

3. **Usage-Based Insurance (UBI)**:

- o Insurance companies offer lower premiums to safe drivers, incentivized through telematics data (International Data Corporation, 2022).

4. **Real-Time Traffic Updates**:

- o Helps drivers avoid accidents, road closures, and hazardous conditions.

4. Public Transportation and Telematics

Telematics is transforming public transit systems, making them safer, greener, and more efficient:

1. **Real-Time Tracking**:

- o Passengers can monitor buses, trains, or taxis via apps for accurate ETAs.

- o **Example**: Singapore's Land Transport Authority uses telematics to provide real-time bus tracking (International Transport Forum, 2022).

2. **Dynamic Scheduling**:

- o Telematics adjusts schedules based on traffic and passenger demand, ensuring optimal resource use.

3. **Eco-Friendly Transit**:

   o Public fleets monitor emissions and promote fuel-efficient driving practices.

4. **Improved Passenger Safety**:

   o Systems track vehicle speeds, driver behavior, and maintenance needs to prevent accidents.

5. Challenges in Telematics Implementation

Despite its advantages, telematics adoption faces several hurdles:

1. **High Initial Costs**:

   o Implementing telematics requires significant investment in hardware, software, and training.

   o **Solution**: Phased implementation and government incentives.

2. **Data Privacy Concerns**:

   o Users are wary of how their data is collected and shared.

   o **Solution**: Transparency in data usage policies and compliance with GDPR regulations (McKinsey & Company, 2021).

3. **Technological Integration**:

   o Legacy systems often struggle to integrate with modern telematics platforms.

   o **Solution**: Standardized APIs streamline integration (International Data Corporation, 2022).

4. **Resistance to Adoption**:

   o Employees may resist telematics due to concerns over surveillance.

   o **Solution**: Education and incentives can build trust and acceptance.

6. Future Trends in Transportation Telematics

Looking ahead, telematics will play a pivotal role in shaping the future of transportation:

1. **Autonomous Vehicles**:

   o Telematics systems will support V2X communication, enabling self-driving cars to interact with traffic systems and other vehicles (Allied Market Research, 2023).

2. **Mobility-as-a-Service (MaaS)**:

   o Integrates multiple transportation modes into unified platforms, offering seamless, eco-friendly travel.

3. **Sustainability Initiatives**:

   o Telematics will drive green practices by reducing emissions and optimizing energy use.

4. **Blockchain Integration**:

   o Ensures secure, transparent data sharing for telematics systems (McKinsey & Company, 2021).

Key Takeaways

• Telematics enhances transportation efficiency, safety, and sustainability.

- Applications include smart vehicles, fleet management, road safety, and public transportation.

- Addressing challenges such as costs and privacy concerns is crucial for widespread adoption.

- Future trends like autonomous vehicles and MaaS will redefine transportation, with telematics at the core.

Chapter 4
Telematics in Urban Environments

Introduction

U rban environments are undergoing a transformation, driven by telematics and the Internet of Things (IoT). Cities worldwide are adopting telematics systems to manage traffic, enhance public safety, and reduce environmental impact. These systems provide real-time insights, enabling cities to optimize resources and improve quality of life for residents.

Consider this: Singapore's telematics-powered dynamic traffic management system has reduced urban commute times by 15%, contributing to a significant decrease in congestion and emissions (International Transport Forum, 2022). This chapter explores how telematics enables smarter urban planning, efficient mobility, and sustainability.

1. Smart Traffic Management

Telematics revolutionizes urban traffic systems by integrating vehicles, infrastructure, and data:

1. **Real-Time Traffic Monitoring**:

    o Sensors and cameras collect data on traffic flow, enabling dynamic adjustments to traffic signals.

    o **Example**: Los Angeles uses telematics to synchronize over 4,000 traffic signals, reducing congestion and travel times (Frost & Sullivan, 2023).

2. **Intelligent Transportation Systems (ITS)**:

   o Telematics connects traffic data with public transit schedules, ensuring efficient coordination.

   o **Example**: Smart highways in the Netherlands use ITS to redirect traffic during peak hours.

3. **Smart Parking**:

   o IoT sensors in parking spaces provide real-time availability updates to drivers via apps.

   o **Case Study**: Barcelona's smart parking system reduced congestion caused by drivers searching for parking, cutting emissions by 30% (Allied Market Research, 2023).

2. Urban Mobility and Shared Transportation

Telematics enables cities to manage mobility more efficiently by supporting shared and sustainable transportation systems:

1. **Ride-Sharing Platforms**:

   o Companies like Uber and Lyft leverage telematics for dynamic pricing, route optimization, and real-time tracking.

2. **Car-Sharing Services**:

   o Telematics tracks vehicle availability and usage patterns, ensuring optimal fleet distribution.

   o **Example**: Zipcar uses telematics to manage vehicle inventory and maintenance schedules.

3. **Micromobility Solutions**:

   o Bike and scooter-sharing platforms use telematics to monitor usage, ensuring availability and safety.

   o **Example**: Lime integrates telematics to provide real-time location data for its electric scooters.

3. Public Safety and Emergency Response

Telematics enhances public safety by providing real-time insights for emergency services and disaster management:

1. **Emergency Vehicle Tracking**:

   o Telematics optimizes routes for ambulances, fire trucks, and police vehicles, reducing response times.

   o **Example**: Tokyo's emergency response system integrates telematics to improve ambulance dispatch by 15% (International Transport Forum, 2022).

2. **Disaster Management**:

   o Real-time data during natural disasters enables coordinated evacuations and resource allocation.

3. **Public Safety Alerts**:

   o Sensors detect hazardous conditions, such as gas leaks or road obstructions, and notify authorities immediately.

4. Environmental Monitoring and Sustainability

Telematics plays a vital role in reducing the environmental footprint of cities:

1. **Air Quality Monitoring**:

    o   IoT sensors measure pollution levels, helping cities implement emission reduction strategies.

    o   **Example**: London uses telematics to enforce Ultra Low Emission Zones (ULEZ), reducing vehicle emissions by 37% (Allied Market Research, 2023).

2. **Energy Efficiency**:

    o   Smart lighting systems adjust brightness based on activity levels, saving energy.

    o   **Example**: Telematics-enabled streetlights in Copenhagen reduced energy consumption by 60% (Frost & Sullivan, 2023).

3. **Waste Management**:

    o   Sensors in waste bins monitor fill levels, optimizing collection routes and reducing fuel consumption.

5. Challenges in Implementing Telematics in Urban Areas

Despite its benefits, implementing telematics in cities faces significant challenges:

1. **High Costs**:

    o   Infrastructure investments for sensors, networks, and platforms can be prohibitive.

    o   **Solution**: Public-private partnerships to share costs.

2. **Interoperability**:

    o   Integrating telematics systems with existing city infrastructure is complex.

- o **Solution**: Adopting standardized protocols and APIs.

3. **Data Privacy and Security**:

    - o Ensuring citizen data is protected from breaches and misuse is critical.

    - o **Solution**: Compliance with global standards like GDPR and encryption of sensitive data.

4. **Resistance to Adoption**:

    - o Legacy systems and organizational resistance can slow implementation.

    - o **Solution**: Demonstrating ROI and providing training for stakeholders.

6. Future Trends in Urban Telematics

1. **Autonomous Public Transit**:

    - o Telematics will power self-driving buses and trains, enhancing urban mobility.

2. **Digital Twins**:

    - o Virtual models of cities will use telematics data for real-time simulations, improving urban planning.

    - o **Example**: Singapore's digital twin integrates telematics to optimize infrastructure development.

3. **Blockchain for Data Sharing**:

    - o Ensures secure and transparent sharing of urban telematics data among stakeholders.

4. **Hyperconnected Ecosystems**:

   o Seamless integration of telematics across public services, transportation, and utilities will create smarter, more efficient cities.

Key Takeaways

- Telematics is integral to smart cities, enabling real-time traffic management, enhanced public safety, and sustainability initiatives.

- It supports shared mobility, dynamic scheduling, and resource optimization.

- Addressing challenges like costs and data privacy is essential for widespread adoption.

- Future trends such as digital twins and hyperconnected ecosystems will further enhance urban environments.

Chapter 5
Beyond Vehicles: Telematics in Other Industries

1. Introduction

Telematics has evolved far beyond its initial applications in transportation, extending its influence into sectors such as healthcare, agriculture, retail, and construction. These industries leverage telematics to optimize operations, improve safety, and enhance decision-making.

Consider this: By 2025, the global telematics market outside of transportation is projected to surpass $50 billion, driven by advancements in IoT and predictive analytics (Frost & Sullivan, 2023). This chapter explores how telematics is revolutionizing diverse industries, the challenges it faces, and the trends shaping its future.

2. Telematics in Healthcare

Telematics is redefining healthcare by enabling real-time monitoring and enhancing patient outcomes:

1. **Remote Patient Monitoring (RPM)**:

   o Wearable devices like smartwatches and health trackers collect vital signs, such as heart rate and oxygen levels, and transmit data to healthcare providers for proactive care.

   o **Example**: Telehealth platforms use telematics data from wearable devices to provide virtual consultations, reducing hospital visits by 25% (McKinsey & Company, 2021).

2. **Emergency Response Systems**:

   o Telematics-equipped ambulances optimize routes, reducing response times during emergencies.

   o **Case Study**: In Tokyo, telematics-enabled ambulances improved response times by 15%, enhancing survival rates for critical patients (International Transport Forum, 2022).

3. **Data-Driven Health Insights**:

   o AI-driven telematics systems analyze patient data to predict chronic conditions or potential health risks, enabling preventive care.

   o **Example**: Hospitals use telematics to track hospital beds and patient movements, improving resource allocation.

3. Telematics in Agriculture

Agriculture leverages telematics to increase productivity, conserve resources, and ensure sustainability:

1. **Precision Farming**:

   o GPS-enabled tractors and sensors monitor soil moisture, crop health, and weather conditions, enabling targeted irrigation and fertilization.

   o **Case Study**: A farm in Iowa using John Deere's telematics reduced water usage by 30% and increased yields by 20% (Frost & Sullivan, 2023).

2. **Livestock Management**:

   o   Telematics monitors the location, health, and behavior of livestock, helping farmers detect diseases early and ensure optimal conditions.

3. **Supply Chain Efficiency**:

   o   Real-time tracking ensures the safe transportation of produce, maintaining quality during transit.

4. **Environmental Impact**:

   o   Sensors track environmental factors like rainfall and soil erosion, helping farmers adopt sustainable practices.

4. Telematics in Retail and Supply Chains

Retail and supply chain operations benefit significantly from telematics, enhancing efficiency and customer satisfaction:

1. **Inventory Tracking**:

   o   Retailers use telematics to monitor inventory levels and optimize stock replenishment in real time.

   o   **Example**: Amazon employs telematics systems to manage its warehouses, reducing delivery delays by 25% (McKinsey & Company, 2021).

2. **Fleet and Logistics Optimization**:

   o   Real-time tracking of delivery vehicles minimizes delays and ensures the safety of goods in transit.

   o   **Case Study**: A global logistics firm reduced fuel costs by 15% using telematics-based fleet monitoring.

3. **Customer Experience**:

   o Personalized updates on delivery status improve customer satisfaction and retention.

5. Telematics in Construction and Heavy Equipment

Telematics enhances the safety, productivity, and sustainability of construction projects:

1. **Equipment Utilization**:

   o Tracks usage patterns of heavy machinery, ensuring optimal deployment and reducing idle time.

   o **Example**: Caterpillar uses telematics to monitor construction equipment, improving project timelines by 20%.

2. **Safety Monitoring**:

   o Sensors detect unsafe operating conditions or equipment malfunctions, preventing accidents.

3. **Fuel and Resource Management**:

   o Tracks fuel consumption and efficiency, promoting eco-friendly practices.

4. **Remote Diagnostics**:

   o Engineers can diagnose equipment issues remotely, minimizing downtime.

6. Challenges

Despite its advantages, telematics adoption in non-transportation industries faces several hurdles:

1. **High Implementation Costs**:

   o Integrating telematics into existing operations requires significant investment in hardware, software, and training.

   o **Solution**: Governments and industry partnerships can subsidize implementation.

2. **Data Privacy Concerns**:

   o Healthcare and retail face stringent regulations regarding sensitive data.

   o **Solution**: Employ encryption and comply with standards like GDPR to build trust.

3. **Legacy System Integration**:

   o Many industries struggle to integrate telematics with outdated systems.

   o **Solution**: APIs and cloud-based platforms simplify integration.

4. **Regulatory Hurdles**:

   o Industries like healthcare and agriculture face unique compliance challenges.

   o **Solution**: Engage with regulators to ensure telematics systems meet industry standards.

7. Future Trends

Telematics is poised to revolutionize even more industries with emerging trends:

1. **Energy Management**:
   - Telematics will optimize energy grids, ensuring efficient distribution and consumption.

2. **Smart Cities**:
   - Integrating telematics across industries will create interconnected urban ecosystems, enhancing the quality of life.

3. **AI-Powered Insights**:
   - Advanced AI will make telematics systems smarter, offering predictive insights across diverse sectors.

4. **Blockchain for Data Security**:
   - Blockchain will ensure transparent and secure telematics data sharing.

5. **Cross-Industry Collaboration**:
   - Sectors like healthcare and retail will collaborate to create integrated telematics solutions, enhancing efficiency.

8. Key Takeaways

- Telematics has expanded beyond vehicles, transforming industries such as healthcare, agriculture, retail, and construction.

- It enhances efficiency, safety, and sustainability while enabling predictive analytics and resource optimization.

- Addressing challenges like high costs and regulatory hurdles is crucial for widespread adoption.

- Emerging trends in energy management, AI, and blockchain will unlock new opportunities for telematics across industries.

Chapter 6
The Role of Data in Telematics

Introduction

Data drives the functionality and intelligence of telematics systems, transforming raw information into actionable insights that improve safety, efficiency, and decision-making. The exponential growth of data has made telematics indispensable in industries like transportation, healthcare, and urban planning.

Consider this: In 2023, telematics systems globally generated over 80 exabytes of data, with projections to exceed 100 exabytes by 2030 (Frost & Sullivan, 2023). This chapter delves into how telematics systems collect, process, and utilize data, addressing privacy concerns, challenges, and emerging trends.

2. Data Collection in Telematics

Telematics systems gather data from diverse sources to provide a comprehensive view of operations:

1. Vehicles

- **What is Collected:** OBD-II systems capture vehicle health metrics such as engine performance, fuel efficiency, and fault codes.

- **Example:** Tesla vehicles continuously collect data on battery performance and driver behavior to improve EV performance (McKinsey & Company, 2021).

2. IoT Sensors

- **What is Collected:** Sensors measure environmental factors (e.g., air quality, humidity) and operational conditions (e.g., tire pressure, cargo temperature).

- **Example:** A trucking company uses IoT sensors to monitor cargo temperature, ensuring perishable goods remain fresh during transit.

3. External Systems

- **What is Collected:** Data from external sources, such as traffic conditions, weather forecasts, and road infrastructure, integrates with vehicle data for enhanced decision-making.

- **Example:** Smart cities incorporate telematics data with real-time traffic updates to adjust signal timings and reduce congestion.

4. Historical vs. Real-Time Data

- **Real-Time:** Enables immediate decisions, such as rerouting vehicles during accidents.

- **Historical:** Supports trend analysis for long-term improvements, such as predicting peak traffic times.

3. Data Processing and Analysis

Once collected, data is processed and analyzed to extract meaningful insights:

1. **Steps in Data Processing**

1. **Data Cleaning:**

   o Removes inaccuracies and redundancies for reliable analysis.

- o **Example:** Removing duplicate location pings from GPS logs.

2. **Data Aggregation:**

   - o Combines data from various sources for a unified view.

   - o **Example:** Merging vehicle diagnostics with real-time traffic data.

3. **Data Analysis:**

   - o Applies algorithms to identify patterns, trends, and anomalies.

2. Types of Analytics

1. **Descriptive Analytics:**

   - o Answers: "What happened?"

   - o **Example:** Identifying that a vehicle's fuel consumption increased by 15% last month.

2. **Predictive Analytics:**

   - o Answers: "What might happen?"

   - o **Example:** Predicting tire wear based on mileage and driving conditions.

3. **Prescriptive Analytics:**

   - o Answers: "What should be done?"

   - o **Example:** Recommending specific routes to reduce delivery times.

3. Case Study

- A global logistics company implemented AI-driven analytics to predict maintenance issues, reducing downtime by 25% (Frost & Sullivan, 2023).

4. Data Utilization

Telematics systems translate raw data into actionable outcomes:

1. Efficiency

- Fleet Optimization: Real-time data helps fleet managers choose the most fuel-efficient routes.

- Example: UPS optimized its delivery routes, reducing annual miles driven by 10 million (McKinsey & Company, 2021).

2. Safety

- Driver Monitoring: Detects risky behaviors such as harsh braking, enabling driver training programs.

- Example: A fleet reduced accidents by 20% after adopting telematics-based safety monitoring.

3. Sustainability

- Emission Monitoring: Tracks fuel usage and carbon emissions to align with sustainability goals.

- Example: A logistics company used telematics to reduce its carbon footprint by 30% (International Transport Forum, 2022).

5. Data Privacy and Security

As telematics systems handle sensitive data, robust privacy and security measures are essential:

1. Privacy Concerns

- Issue: Monitoring driver behavior and vehicle locations raises ethical questions.

- Solution: Transparency in data usage policies, allowing users to control data sharing.

2. Security Risks

- Issue: Connected systems are vulnerable to hacking and data breaches.

- Solution: Implementing encryption protocols and firewalls.

- Example: Blockchain secures telematics data, ensuring tamper-proof storage (Allied Market Research, 2023).

3. Regulatory Compliance

- Standards: GDPR and CCPA require telematics systems to prioritize user consent and data protection.

6. Challenges in Managing Telematics Data

While telematics data offers immense value, it comes with challenges:

1. Data Overload

- Issue: Processing vast data volumes in real time strains infrastructure.

- Solution: Edge computing processes data locally, reducing latency.

2. Integration with Legacy Systems

- Issue: Outdated systems often lack compatibility with modern telematics platforms.

- Solution: APIs and cloud integration services streamline data flows.

3. Cost of Infrastructure

- Issue: Managing robust telematics systems requires substantial investment.

- Solution: Scalable cloud-based solutions reduce upfront costs.

7. Future Trends in Data Utilization

Emerging technologies are set to revolutionize telematics data management:

1. AI and Machine Learning

- Advances: AI will enhance predictive accuracy, identifying trends that improve decision-making.

- Example: Predicting traffic patterns to optimize urban planning.

2. Edge Computing

Impact: Processes data locally, enabling faster decision-making.

- **Example:** Autonomous vehicles use edge computing for obstacle detection and navigation.

3. Collaborative Data Ecosystems

- **Potential:** Industries will share anonymized data for mutual benefits, such as improving smart city systems.

4. Blockchain Integration

- **Benefit:** Provides secure, transparent data sharing across stakeholders.

8. Key Takeaways

- Data is central to telematics, powering real-time insights and predictive analytics.

- Challenges like data overload and privacy concerns require innovative solutions like edge computing and blockchain.

- Future trends, including AI-driven analytics and collaborative data ecosystems, will unlock new possibilities for telematics.

Chapter 7
Cybersecurity in the Telematics Era

Introduction

With the increasing adoption of telematics across industries, cybersecurity has become a critical concern. Telematics systems, which rely on connected devices and IoT ecosystems, handle vast amounts of sensitive data—making them attractive targets for cybercriminals.

Consider this: A ransomware attack in 2022 targeted a global logistics company's telematics platform, halting operations for days and resulting in millions of dollars in losses (Frost & Sullivan, 2023). As telematics systems expand in scope, ensuring their security is paramount for protecting data integrity, privacy, and operational continuity.

This chapter explores the cybersecurity threats facing telematics systems, strategies to mitigate these risks, global regulations, and emerging challenges.

2. Threats and Vulnerabilities

Telematics systems face a variety of cybersecurity threats. Understanding these vulnerabilities is the first step toward mitigating them.

1. GPS Signal Spoofing

- **How It Works**: Hackers manipulate GPS signals to mislead telematics systems, causing vehicles to navigate to incorrect locations.

Impact:

- o Fleet disruptions.

- o Increased risk of cargo theft.

- **Example**: A 2019 incident in the Black Sea saw multiple vessels report erroneous GPS coordinates, attributed to signal spoofing (International Transport Forum, 2022).

2. Ransomware Attacks

- **How It Works**: Malicious actors lock telematics systems and demand payment for decryption keys.

- **Impact**:

  - o Operational downtime.

  - o Financial and reputational damage.

- **Example**: A fleet management company lost access to its telematics dashboard, causing delays in shipments for several weeks.

3. Data Breaches

- **How It Works**: Unauthorized access to telematics platforms exposes sensitive data, including vehicle locations, driver behaviors, and operational logs.

- **Impact**:

  - o Loss of customer trust.

  - o Regulatory penalties under GDPR or CCPA.

Example: A major automaker faced a data breach in 2021 that compromised vehicle tracking information of over 20,000 users.

4. IoT Device Vulnerabilities

- **How It Works**: IoT sensors and devices often lack robust security, making them entry points for attackers.

- **Impact**:

  o Spread of malware across connected systems.

  o Compromise of core telematics functionalities.

5. Integration Risks

- **How It Works**: Legacy systems connected to modern telematics platforms create vulnerabilities.

- **Impact**:

  o Weakens overall security.

  o Complicates incident response.

3. Strategies for Safeguarding Telematics Systems

Securing telematics systems requires a multi-pronged approach combining technological, procedural, and regulatory measures.

1. Encryption

- **Role**: Protects data in transit and at rest using robust protocols like AES-256.

  - **Example**: Encrypted GPS signals thwart spoofing attempts and prevent unauthorized location tracking.

2. Blockchain for Data Security

- **Role**: Provides decentralized, tamper-proof storage for sensitive data.

- **Example**: A fleet management company uses blockchain to secure vehicle usage logs, ensuring data integrity during audits.

3. Regular Software Updates

- **Role**: Patches vulnerabilities in telematics systems and connected devices.

- **Example**: Over-the-air (OTA) updates for connected vehicles prevent known exploits.

4. AI-Powered Threat Detection

- **Role**: Identifies anomalies in system behavior, such as unusual data flows or login attempts.

- **Example**: AI detected a distributed denial-of-service (DDoS) attack on a telematics platform, preventing significant downtime.

5. Multi-Factor Authentication (MFA)

- **Role**: Strengthens user authentication by requiring multiple credentials, such as passwords and biometric verification.

6. Secure IoT Devices

- **Role**: Incorporates security protocols into IoT devices, reducing vulnerabilities.

- **Example:** IoT-enabled trucks use device-level encryption to secure communication with central systems.

4. Global Standards and Regulations

Adherence to global standards ensures robust cybersecurity while maintaining compliance with legal frameworks:

- **General Data Protection Regulation (GDPR)**

- **Region**: European Union.

- **Focus**: Protects personal data and mandates transparent data usage policies.

2. California Consumer Privacy Act (CCPA)

- **Region**: United States (California).

- **Focus**: Grants consumers control over their data, including rights to access and delete information.

3. UNECE WP.29 Cybersecurity Regulation

- **Region**: International.

- **Focus**: Establishes cybersecurity protocols for connected vehicles to ensure data integrity and resilience.

4. ISO 27001

- **Focus**: Provides a framework for implementing an effective information security management system.

5. NHTSA Guidelines

- **Region**: United States

- **Focus**: Offers best practices for automotive cybersecurity, including secure software development and intrusion detection.

5. Emerging Challenges

As telematics systems evolve, so do the cybersecurity threats they face:

1. AI-Driven Cyberattacks

- **Threat**: Attackers use AI to automate and scale attacks, such as generating phishing emails or exploiting vulnerabilities.

- **Impact**: Accelerated attack timelines and increased success rates.

2. Quantum Computing

- **Threat**: Quantum computing could render current encryption methods obsolete, necessitating quantum-resistant algorithms.

- **Solution**: Research into post-quantum cryptography is underway.

3. IoT Expansion

- **Threat**: The proliferation of IoT devices increases attack surfaces, making centralized control more challenging.

- **Solution**: IoT security protocols like TLS (Transport Layer Security) ensure secure device communication.

4. Supply Chain Risks

- **Threat**: Cyberattacks on third-party vendors can compromise entire telematics ecosystems.

- **Solution**: Conduct regular security audits of suppliers.

6. Case Study: Securing a Fleet Management System

Background: A global logistics provider experienced frequent cyberattacks targeting its telematics platform, leading to operational disruptions.

Solution: The company implemented a multi-layered security strategy:

1. **End-to-End Encryption**: Protected data from unauthorized access.

2. **AI Threat Detection**: Monitored real-time activity to detect anomalies.

3. **Blockchain for Data Integrity**: Secured records of vehicle maintenance and usage. **Results**:

- Reduced cyber incidents by 40%.

- Increased customer trust due to enhanced data security.

7. Key Takeaways

- Cybersecurity is a cornerstone of telematics, protecting data integrity, privacy, and operational efficiency.

- Common threats include GPS spoofing, ransomware, and data breaches, all requiring robust countermeasures.

- Strategies like encryption, AI-driven threat detection, and blockchain integration enhance security.

- Adherence to global standards (e.g., GDPR, UNECE WP.29) ensures compliance and user trust.

- Future challenges like AI-driven attacks and quantum computing demand proactive solutions to maintain secure telematics ecosystems.

Chapter 8 Emerging Technologies Driving Telematics

Introduction

Emerging technologies are revolutionizing telematics by unlocking new possibilities for connectivity, analytics, and security. As industries adopt advanced tools like 5G, AI, and blockchain, telematics systems are transforming into smarter, faster, and more reliable platforms.

Consider this: By 2030, emerging technologies like AI and 5G will enable telematics systems to process over 200 exabytes of data annually, driving innovation across autonomous vehicles, logistics, and urban planning (Allied Market Research, 2023). This chapter explores how these technologies are shaping the future of telematics and their potential for further transformation.

2. 5G Connectivity

Transforming Telematics with 5G

5G networks deliver unprecedented speed, capacity, and reliability, making them foundational for advanced telematics applications.

1. **Ultra-Low Latency**:

   o Enables real-time data exchange critical for autonomous vehicles and advanced driver assistance systems (ADAS).

   o **Example**: Tesla's self-driving systems use 5G to process data from sensors and cameras instantly, ensuring safe navigation.

2. **Massive Data Throughput**:

   o Handles the high data volumes generated by IoT sensors, video feeds, and vehicle diagnostics.

   o **Example**: Logistics companies use 5G to monitor fleet performance in real time, reducing downtime and enhancing efficiency.

3. **Reliable V2X Communication**:

   o Supports seamless communication between vehicles, infrastructure, and pedestrians.

   o **Example**: Smart cities like Singapore leverage 5G to synchronize traffic lights based on real-time vehicle density, reducing congestion by 25%.

4. **Enhanced Remote Operations**:

   o Enables telematics systems to support remote vehicle diagnostics and over-the-air (OTA) updates.

3. Artificial Intelligence (AI)

The Intelligence Behind Modern Telematics

AI enables telematics systems to go beyond monitoring, providing predictive insights and adaptive responses.

1. **Predictive Maintenance**:

   o AI algorithms analyze historical and real-time data to predict mechanical failures before they occur.

   o **Example**: A rucking company reduced breakdowns by 30% using AI-driven telematics to monitor engine health (McKinsey&Company, 2021).

2. **Dynamic Routing**:

   o AI optimizes delivery routes by considering traffic patterns, weather conditions, and fuel efficiency.

   o **Example**: FedEx integrated AI into its telematics system to cut delivery times by 15% during peak seasons.

3. **Driver Behavior Analysis**:

   o Monitors metrics like acceleration, braking, and cornering to enhance driver safety.

   o **Example**: Insurance providers use AI-driven telematics to reward safe driving with reduced premiums.

4. **Real-Time Decision Making**:

   o AI powers ADAS features like lane-keeping assist and collision avoidance.

   o **Example**: Mercedes-Benz uses AI to detect and respond to potential hazards in milliseconds.

4. Edge Computing

Enabling Real-Time Data Processing

Edge computing processes data closer to its source, reducing latency and bandwidth requirements while enhancing system resilience.

1. **Localized Decision-Making**:

   o Autonomous vehicles analyze sensor data locally to make immediate decisions, such as avoiding obstacles.

o **Example**: A connected car detects a pedestrian and applies brakes instantly without relying on cloudbased systems.

2. **Optimized Resource Utilization**:

   o Reduces dependency on centralized cloud servers, lowering operational costs.

   o **Example**: Fleet operators use edge devices to analyze fuel consumption data in real time.

3. **Improved Security**:

   o Limits exposure of sensitive data to external networks, reducing cybersecurity risks.

4. **Application in Remote Areas**:

   o Ensures reliable telematics performance in locations with limited network connectivity.

5. Blockchain

Building Trust and Security

Blockchain enhances telematics by ensuring data integrity, transparency, and security.

1. **Data Integrity**:

   o Ensures that telematics data is tamper-proof and verifiable.

   o **Example**: Blockchain secures maintenance records, enabling transparent audits for fleet operators.

2. **Decentralized Ecosystems**:

- o Eliminates reliance on centralized servers, reducing single points of failure.

- o **Example**: A logistics company uses blockchain to securely share shipment data across stakeholders, ensuring accountability.

3. **Secure Smart Contracts**:

- o Automates transactions, such as insurance claims, based on predefined conditions.

- o **Example**: Usage-based insurance leverages blockchain to verify driving data and process claims automatically.

4. **Enhanced Privacy Controls**:

- o Empowers users to control who accesses their data, mitigating privacy concerns.

6. Vehicle-to-Everything (V2X) Communication

Creating Hyperconnected Ecosystems

V2X communication connects vehicles to their environment, enabling safer and more efficient transportation systems.

1. **Vehicle-to-Vehicle (V2V)**:

- o Vehicles share data like speed, location, and braking patterns to prevent collisions.

- o **Example**: Honda's V2V systems alert nearby cars of sudden stops, improving highway safety.

2. **Vehicle-to-Infrastructure (V2I)**:

- o Integrates vehicles with traffic lights, toll systems, and parking facilities to streamline operations.

- o **Example**: Smart intersections in Los Angeles adjust signal timings dynamically based on V2I data.

3. **Vehicle-to-Pedestrian (V2P)**:

- o Enhances pedestrian safety by alerting vehicles of nearby individuals through smartphones or wearable devices.

7. Future Trends

1. Quantum Computing

- **Opportunities**: Solves complex optimization problems, such as dynamic fleet routing, in real time.

- **Challenges**: Existing encryption methods may become obsolete, requiring quantum-resistant algorithms.

2. Collaborative Data Ecosystems

- **Vision**: Industries share anonymized telematics data to enhance urban mobility and smart city planning.

- **Example**: A city collaborates with logistics companies to optimize traffic flow using shared telematics insights.

3. IoT Expansion

- **Impact**: Integration of billions of IoT devices will create hyperconnected systems, from autonomous vehicles to energy grids.

4. Sustainability Initiatives

- **Advancements**: Telematics systems will play a crucial role in reducing emissions, optimizing fuel usage, and promoting green technologies.

8. Key Takeaways

- Emerging technologies like 5G, AI, edge computing, and blockchain are redefining telematics, enabling real-time insights, predictive analytics, and enhanced security.

- V2X communication creates hyperconnected ecosystems, improving safety and operational efficiency.

- Future trends like quantum computing and collaborative data ecosystems promise to unlock new possibilities for telematics.

Adapting to these advancements is essential for organizations to remain competitive in a connected world.

Chapter 9 Telematics and Sustainability

Introduction

Telematics is transforming sustainability initiatives by enabling smarter resource utilization, reducing emissions, and optimizing operations. As global industries aim to achieve net-zero emissions and align with the UN's Sustainable Development Goals (SDGs), telematics has emerged as a pivotal technology in this journey.

Consider this: In 2022, telematics systems saved logistics companies over 10 million metric tons of CO_2 emissions globally through route optimization and idle-time monitoring (Allied Market Research, 2023). This chapter explores how telematics is driving sustainability across industries and contributing to environmental, operational, and social well-being.

2. Environmental Impact of Telematics

1. Emissions Reduction

- **Telematics systems monitor vehicle performance and driver behavior to reduce fuel consumption and carbon emissions.**

- **Example: A global trucking fleet implemented telematics to optimize routes and monitor idle times, cutting emissions by 30% annually (McKinsey & Company, 2021).**

2. Resource Conservation

Water Management in Agriculture:

- **Telematics-driven IoT sensors monitor soil moisture levels and adjust irrigation schedules.**

- o **Example: Farms in California reduced water usage by 25% while maintaining crop yields using precision farming technologies.**

- **Energy Optimization in Urban Areas:**

  - o **Smart grids leverage telematics to balance energy loads and prioritize renewable sources.**

3. Monitoring Air Quality

- **IoT-enabled telematics systems track pollution levels in real time, enabling cities to implement targeted interventions.**

- **Example: London's Ultra Low Emission Zone (ULEZ) uses telematics to enforce clean air policies, reducing nitrogen oxide levels by 37%.**

3. Operational Sustainability

1. Fuel Efficiency

- **Fleet managers use telematics to analyze driving behaviors like harsh braking or speeding, which directly impact fuel consumption.**

- **Example: UPS leveraged telematics to save 10 million gallons of fuel annually through dynamic routing and idle-time monitoring (Frost & Sullivan, 2023).**

2. Waste Reduction

Supply Chain Optimization:

- o **Telematics minimizes overstock and reduces waste by optimizing delivery schedules.**

- o Example: A retail giant reduced food spoilage by 20% by using telematics to monitor delivery conditions.

- Construction Waste:

  - o Heavy equipment fleets use telematics to monitor material usage, reducing wastage on large-scale projects.

3. Predictive Maintenance

- Telematics enables early detection of equipment issues, reducing the need for frequent replacements and repairs.

- Example: A mining company reduced machinery downtime by 25% through telematics-enabled maintenance alerts.

4. Social and Economic Contributions

1. Enhanced Safety

- Telematics systems monitor driver behavior and provide real-time alerts, significantly reducing accidents.

- Example: A logistics company reduced collisions by 40% after implementing telematics to monitor risky driving behaviors.

2. Job Creation

The telematics industry is creating new opportunities in software development, data analytics, and fleet management.

3. Equity in Urban Mobility

- Smart cities use telematics to create equitable transportation systems by integrating data from public transit, bike-sharing programs, and pedestrian pathways.

5. Telematics in Renewable Energy and EVs

1. EV Fleet Management

- **Telematics systems optimize battery usage, charging schedules, and route planning for electric vehicles (EVs).**

- **Example: A delivery fleet extended EV battery life by 15% using predictive analytics.**

2. Renewable Energy Integration ⏹ Smart Grids:

- o **Telematics integrates renewable energy sources like solar and wind into energy grids, optimizing supply-demand balance.**

- o **Example: A smart city in Denmark uses telematics to manage energy loads, prioritizing renewable sources during peak hours.**

6. Future Trends in Sustainability

1. Circular Economy

- **Resource Reuse:**

  - o Telematics tracks material flows to facilitate recycling and reuse in industries like construction and manufacturing.

      o   Example: A manufacturing plant used telematics to identify and recycle 80% of its scrap materials.

2. Smart Cities

- Telematics systems in smart cities enable eco-friendly urban planning by monitoring traffic emissions, air quality, and waste management.

3. Autonomous and Connected Vehicles

- Self-driving fleets leverage telematics to optimize energy usage and reduce emissions, accelerating sustainability goals.

4. Climate Resilience

- Telematics provides real-time data to predict and mitigate climate-related risks, such as floods or extreme weather conditions.

7. Challenges and Solutions

1. High Implementation Costs

- Challenge: Smaller companies face barriers due to the initial investment in telematics systems.

- Solution: Governments and NGOs can provide subsidies or tax incentives for adopting telematics.

2. Resistance to Change

- Challenge: Operators and employees may be reluctant to adopt new technologies.

- Solution: Training programs and clear demonstrations of ROI can address concerns.

3. Data Privacy Concerns

- Challenge: Balancing sustainability initiatives with data protection laws like GDPR.

- Solution: Implement robust encryption and transparent data-sharing policies.

4. Integration with Legacy Systems

- Challenge: Older infrastructure may not seamlessly connect with modern telematics platforms.

- Solution: Use middleware solutions to bridge compatibility gaps.

8. Key Takeaways

- Telematics plays a pivotal role in achieving sustainability by reducing emissions, conserving resources, and optimizing operations.

- The technology's environmental, operational, and social contributions align with global sustainability goals, such as net-zero emissions.

- Challenges like high costs and data privacy concerns require innovative solutions, including government support and advanced encryption.

- Future trends like autonomous vehicles, smart cities, and the circular economy will further enhance telematics' impact on sustainability.

Chapter 10 The Future of Telematics

Introduction

Telematics has evolved from simple vehicle tracking systems to a critical enabler of smart, connected ecosystems across industries. As emerging technologies like AI, IoT, and blockchain converge, telematics is poised to redefine the future of connectivity, efficiency, and sustainability.

Consider this: By 2035, the telematics industry is projected to reach $400 billion, driven by advancements in autonomous vehicles, smart cities, and data-driven decision-making (Frost & Sullivan, 2023). This chapter explores the transformative potential of emerging technologies in telematics and the challenges and opportunities they present.

2. AI and Machine Learning

AI and machine learning (ML) are at the core of modern telematics, enabling predictive analytics, real-time decisionmaking, and system optimization.

1. **Predictive Maintenance**:

    o AI models analyze historical and real-time data to predict equipment failures and maintenance needs.

    o **Example**: Logistics fleets reduced downtime by 25% using AI to monitor engine health and detect wear patterns (McKinsey & Company, 2021).

2. **Dynamic Routing**:

    AI calculates optimal delivery routes by considering traffic, weather, and fuel efficiency.

- o **Example**: A courier service cut delivery times by 30% during peak seasons using AI-driven routing algorithms.

3. **Driver Behavior Analysis**:

   - o AI monitors driving behaviors like speed, braking, and cornering to promote safety and efficiency.

   - o **Example**: Insurance companies reward safe drivers with lower premiums using telematics-powered AI analytics.

4. **Real-Time Decision Making**:

   - o Autonomous systems leverage AI to interpret sensor data and make split-second decisions.

   - o **Example**: Tesla's Full Self-Driving (FSD) software processes 70,000 data points per second to ensure vehicle safety.

3. IoT Expansion and Hyperconnected Ecosystems

The Internet of Things (IoT) is expanding rapidly, connecting billions of devices to create hyperconnected ecosystems.

1. **Vehicle and Infrastructure Integration**:

   - o IoT sensors in vehicles, roads, and traffic systems enable seamless communication.

   Example: Smart intersections in Singapore use IoTenabled telematics to reduce traffic congestion by 25%.

2. **Remote Monitoring and Control**:

  ○ IoT devices allow fleet managers to monitor vehicles, cargo, and routes in real time.

  ○ **Example**: Cold chain logistics companies ensure temperature-sensitive goods remain within safe ranges using IoT-enabled telematics.

3. **Scalability**:

  ○ IoT ecosystems will support billions of devices, enabling new use cases like connected EV charging stations and urban energy grids.

4. Blockchain for Secure Data Sharing

Blockchain technology is revolutionizing data security and transparency in telematics systems.

1. **Data Integrity**:

  ○ Blockchain ensures telematics data is tamper-proof and traceable.

  ○ **Example**: Insurance companies use blockchain to verify driving data for usage-based insurance claims.

2. **Decentralized Ecosystems**:

  ○ Blockchain eliminates reliance on central servers, reducing single points of failure.

  Example: A logistics firm shares verified shipment data across stakeholders using blockchain.

3. **Smart Contracts**:

- o Automates processes like payments and claims based on predefined conditions.

- o **Example**: Smart contracts automatically release payments when cargo reaches its destination.

4. **Privacy Controls**:

- o Allows users to control access to their telematics data, addressing privacy concerns.

5. 5G and Beyond

5G networks and future advancements like 6G are revolutionizing telematics by enabling faster, more reliable data transmission.

1. **Ultra-Low Latency**:

- o Critical for real-time applications like autonomous driving and V2X communication.

- o **Example**: Self-driving vehicles use 5G to process sensor data and navigate safely in complex environments.

2. **Massive Data Handling**:

- o Supports high data volumes from IoT devices, cameras, and vehicle diagnostics.

- o **Example**: Logistics companies use 5G to analyze fleet performance across global operations.

3. **Enhanced V2X Communication**:

- o Connects vehicles to infrastructure, pedestrians, and other vehicles for safer roads.

- o **Example**: Smart cities synchronize traffic lights using 5G-enabled V2X systems, improving traffic flow.

6. Quantum Computing's Role

Quantum computing will unlock unprecedented capabilities for telematics while posing significant challenges to data security.

1. **Opportunities**:

    o Solves complex optimization problems, such as fleet routing, in real time.

    o **Example**: Quantum algorithms can optimize delivery schedules for thousands of vehicles in seconds.

2. **Challenges**:

    o Existing encryption methods may become obsolete, necessitating quantum-resistant cryptography.

7. Telematics and Sustainability

Telematics systems will play a pivotal role in achieving sustainability goals by reducing emissions, conserving resources, and supporting renewable energy integration.

1. **EV Fleet Management**:

    o Telematics optimizes EV charging schedules, battery performance, and energy usage.

    o **Example**: An EV fleet operator extended battery life by 20% using predictive analytics.

2. **Smart Cities**:

    o Telematics integrates with IoT to monitor air quality, optimize public transportation, and reduce energy waste.

3. **Renewable Energy Grids**:

   o Telematics helps balance energy loads in grids, prioritizing renewable sources like solar and wind.

8. Challenges and Solutions

1. **Data Privacy Concerns**:

   o **Challenge**: Increasing data collection raises risks of misuse.

   o **Solution**: Implement advanced encryption and adhere to regulations like GDPR.

2. **IoT Scalability**:

   o **Challenge**: Managing billions of devices across telematics ecosystems.

   o **Solution**: Use edge computing and distributed networks for scalability.

3. **Resistance to Adoption**:

   o **Challenge**: Stakeholders may resist telematics adoption due to costs or perceived complexity.

   o **Solution**: Highlight ROI through pilot programs and training.

4. **Quantum Threats**:

   o **Challenge**: Quantum computing could undermine current encryption methods.

   o **Solution**: Invest in quantum-resistant cryptographic standards.

9. Case Studies

1. **Smart City Integration**:

   o A city in Scandinavia reduced traffic congestion by 40% using AI-powered telematics systems.

2. **Fleet Optimization**:

   o A logistics company used blockchain to improve shipment tracking and reduce insurance disputes by 50%.

3. **EV Fleet Management**:

   o A delivery fleet extended battery life by leveraging real-time telematics analytics.

10. Key Takeaways

- Emerging technologies like AI, IoT, blockchain, and quantum computing are redefining telematics' potential across industries.

  Addressing challenges like privacy concerns and IoT scalability is critical for widespread adoption.

- Telematics systems will play a central role in advancing sustainability goals, from reducing emissions to supporting renewable energy.

- Businesses and policymakers must proactively embrace these advancements to remain competitive in a hyperconnected world.

Chapter 11 Challenges and Opportunities in Telematics

Introduction

Telematics systems are rapidly transforming industries by enabling connectivity, data-driven decision-making, and operational efficiency. However, with these advancements come significant challenges that must be addressed to unlock their full potential.

Consider this: By 2030, the global telematics market is expected to exceed $400 billion, driven by advancements in autonomous vehicles, IoT ecosystems, and smart cities (Allied Market Research, 2023). This growth brings complex challenges, such as scaling IoT infrastructure and addressing data privacy concerns, alongside unparalleled opportunities for innovation.

2. Challenges in Telematics

The adoption of telematics is hindered by several key challenges:

1. Data Privacy and Security

- Challenge: Telematics systems collect vast amounts of sensitive data, raising concerns about unauthorized access and misuse.

- Impact: Data breaches can erode trust and lead to regulatory penalties.

  Example: A telematics breach in 2022 exposed the location data of over 20,000 vehicles, highlighting the need for robust encryption.

- Solution: Implement end-to-end encryption and compliance with GDPR, CCPA, and other global standards.

2. Cybersecurity Threats

- Challenge: IoT-enabled telematics systems are vulnerable to malware, ransomware, and spoofing attacks.

- Impact: Cyberattacks can disrupt operations, compromise safety, and incur financial losses.

- Example: A ransomware attack on a logistics company's telematics system in 2021 delayed deliveries for weeks.

- Solution: Deploy multi-layered security protocols and AIpowered threat detection tools.

3. Infrastructure Costs

- Challenge: High implementation costs deter small and medium enterprises (SMEs) from adopting telematics.

- Impact: Limits widespread adoption in cost-sensitive industries.

- Solution: Public-private partnerships and scalable cloudbased solutions reduce initial investments.

4. Legacy System Integration

- Challenge: Older infrastructure often lacks compatibility with modern telematics platforms.

  Impact: Hinders the seamless flow of data and operational efficiency.

- Solution: Middleware solutions and standardized APIs facilitate integration.

5. Workforce Readiness

- **Challenge: Adopting telematics requires upskilling employees in data analytics, IoT, and system management.**

- **Impact: Lack of expertise slows adoption and limits ROI.**

- **Solution: Develop training programs and collaborate with educational institutions to create a talent pipeline.**

3. Opportunities in Telematics

Despite these challenges, telematics offers transformative opportunities across industries:

1. Autonomous Systems

- **Opportunity: Telematics serves as the foundation for autonomous vehicles and drones, enabling real-time decision-making.**

- **Example: Self-driving delivery vehicles use telematics to navigate routes efficiently, reducing delivery times by 40%.**

2. Sustainability Initiatives

Opportunity: Telematics systems optimize resource usage, reduce emissions, and promote renewable energy adoption.

- **Example: EV fleets leverage telematics to extend battery life and optimize charging schedules, cutting operational costs by 20% (McKinsey & Company, 2021).**

3. Connected Ecosystems

- **Opportunity: Telematics integrates vehicles, infrastructure, and IoT devices to create hyperconnected smart cities.**

- Example: A smart city in Europe synchronized its public transport systems with real-time traffic data, reducing commute times by 25%.

4. Predictive Analytics

- Opportunity: Businesses use telematics data to forecast trends and proactively address operational challenges.
- Example: Fleet managers reduced maintenance costs by 30% using predictive analytics to schedule repairs.

5. Global Collaboration

- Opportunity: Sharing anonymized telematics data across industries accelerates innovation and improves efficiency.
- Example: Logistics companies collaborate with urban planners to optimize traffic flow and reduce emissions.

4. Actionable Frameworks

1. Overcoming Challenges

- Data Privacy and Security:
  - Action: Adopt advanced encryption protocols and blockchain technology.
  - Result: Enhanced trust and compliance with global regulations.
- Infrastructure Costs:
  - Action: Phase telematics implementation and leverage government subsidies.
  - Result: Improved affordability for SMEs.

- **Workforce Readiness:**

  - o Action: Establish certification programs for telematics professionals.

  - o Result: A skilled workforce ready to maximize telematics potential.

2. Leveraging Opportunities

- **Autonomous Systems:**

  - o Action: Invest in AI-driven telematics systems to support autonomous fleets.

  - o Result: Improved operational efficiency and reduced human error.

- **Sustainability:**

  - o Action: Integrate telematics with renewable energy systems and circular economy practices.

  - o Result: Reduced environmental impact and alignment with global sustainability goals.

5. Case Studies

1. Fleet Optimization

- **Background:** A logistics company faced high fuel costs and inefficient routing.

- **Solution:** Implemented telematics-powered predictive analytics and dynamic routing.

- **Result:** Reduced fuel consumption by 20% and improved delivery times by 30%.

2. Smart City Integration

- **Background: A European city struggled with traffic congestion and public transport delays.**

- **Solution: Integrated telematics with IoT sensors to monitor traffic and optimize transit schedules.**

- **Result: Reduced congestion by 40% and increased public transit efficiency.**

3. Sustainability in Agriculture

- **Background: Farms faced water shortages and rising operational costs.**

- **Solution: Deployed telematics-enabled IoT sensors to monitor soil moisture and automate irrigation.**

  Result: Conserved 30% of water while improving crop yields.

6. Key Takeaways

- **Telematics offers transformative potential but requires addressing challenges like data privacy, cybersecurity, and infrastructure costs.**

- **Key opportunities include autonomous systems, sustainability, predictive analytics, and connected ecosystems.**

- **Collaborative efforts between businesses, governments, and educational institutions are critical to overcoming barriers and maximizing the impact of telematics.**

- **Proactively addressing emerging challenges ensures long-term growth and success in a rapidly evolving telematics landscape.**

Chapter 12 Telematics in a Global Context

Introduction

Telematics is no longer confined to local or industry-specific applications. Its transformative potential spans continents, industries, and economies, making it a cornerstone of global connectivity and sustainability efforts. From streamlining cross-border logistics to enabling climate resilience, telematics is driving a new era of global innovation.

Consider this: By 2035, telematics is expected to power 70% of global logistics operations, generating $500 billion in annual economic value while contributing significantly to sustainability goals (Allied Market Research, 2023). This chapter explores regional variations, global challenges, and opportunities for telematics as it reshapes industries worldwide.

2. Regional Variations in Telematics Adoption

Telematics adoption varies significantly across regions due to differences in infrastructure, regulatory environments, and market needs.

1. North America

- **Strengths**: Advanced infrastructure, strong regulatory frameworks (e.g., FMCSA mandates for electronic logging devices).

- **Example**: U.S. logistics companies use telematics to optimize long-haul trucking routes, saving $10 billion annually.

  Focus: Increasing fleet efficiency and ensuring regulatory compliance.

2. Europe

- **Strengths**: Sustainability focus, GDPR compliance, and widespread adoption of smart city technologies.

- **Example**: Scandinavian cities use telematics to monitor air quality and manage traffic emissions, reducing urban pollution by 30%.

- **Focus**: Integrating telematics into urban planning and environmental policies.

3. Asia-Pacific

- **Strengths**: Rapid growth in telematics for urban mobility and fleet management, driven by dense populations and urbanization.

- **Example**: Japan integrates telematics with vehicle-toeverything (V2X) communication for autonomous vehicle testing.

- **Focus**: Expanding telematics in public transit and autonomous systems.

4. Developing Economies

- **Challenges**: Limited infrastructure, high costs, and regulatory gaps.

- **Example**: In parts of Africa, telematics supports agricultural logistics, improving food supply chains.

- **Focus**: Leveraging telematics for resource optimization and economic development.

3. Global Standards and Regulatory Frameworks

Adherence to international standards is critical for ensuring seamless telematics adoption and data security across borders.

Key Frameworks

1. **General Data Protection Regulation (GDPR)**:

   o Protects personal data and sets a benchmark for privacy regulations globally.

   o **Impact**: Encourages transparency and accountability in telematics systems.

2. **UNECE WP.29 Cybersecurity Regulation**:

   o Establishes cybersecurity protocols for connected vehicles, ensuring data integrity.

   o **Impact**: Enhances trust in telematics systems.

3. **North American ELD Mandates**:

   o Require fleet operators to track driving hours digitally, improving safety and compliance.

4. **ISO 27001**:

   o Provides a framework for information security management systems.

Challenges

Regulatory discrepancies across regions complicate telematics implementations.

☐ **Solution**: Harmonize global standards through international collaboration and trade agreements.

4. Collaboration Across Borders

Global challenges such as climate change, cross-border logistics, and disaster management require international cooperation in telematics adoption.

1. Data Sharing Across Regions

- **Vision**: Enable cross-border logistics optimization through shared telematics data.

- **Example**: European and Asian logistics firms collaborate to streamline transportation networks, reducing delivery times and emissions.

2. Smart Cities as Global Models

- Cities like Singapore and Copenhagen set benchmarks in telematics-driven urban mobility and environmental management.

3. Role of Multinational Corporations

- Companies like DHL and Tesla drive telematics adoption worldwide, creating scalable solutions for diverse markets.

5. Addressing Global Challenges with Telematics

Telematics is uniquely positioned to tackle critical global issues:

1. Climate Change

- **Application**: Monitor and reduce carbon emissions through optimized fleet operations.

- **Example**: A global shipping firm cut its carbon footprint by 25% using telematics-based fuel monitoring.

2. Cross-Border Logistics

- **Application**: Enable real-time tracking and predictive analytics to streamline international supply chains.

- **Example**: Multinational logistics firms reduced border delays by 20% using telematics.

3. Disaster Management

- **Application**: Use telematics to coordinate rescue operations and allocate resources during emergencies.

- **Example**: During a major flood in Southeast Asia, telematics systems accelerated relief efforts by tracking rescue vehicles and supplies.

6. Future Trends in Global Telematics

1. Expansion of IoT Ecosystems

- Growth in IoT devices will enable seamless telematics integration across industries and regions.

2. AI and Predictive Analytics

- AI-driven models will enhance decision-making for crossborder logistics, urban mobility, and energy management.

3. Quantum Computing

  Quantum algorithms will optimize global logistics networks and solve complex operational challenges in seconds.

4. Global Sustainability Goals

- Telematics will play a central role in achieving net-zero emissions and promoting renewable energy integration worldwide.

7. Challenges and Solutions

1. Regulatory Discrepancies

- **Challenge**: Regional variations in telematics regulations create barriers to global implementation.
- **Solution**: Harmonize international policies through organizations like ISO and UNECE.

2. Infrastructure Gaps

- **Challenge**: Developing economies face limited access to reliable connectivity.
- **Solution**: Public-private partnerships can fund infrastructure development and telematics deployment.

3. Data Privacy Concerns

- **Challenge**: Cross-border data sharing raises compliance issues.
- **Solution**: Blockchain ensures secure and transparent data exchanges.

4. Resistance to Change

Challenge: Businesses may resist telematics adoption due to perceived complexity.

- **Solution**: Demonstrate ROI through pilot programs and training initiatives.

8. Case Studies

1. Cross-Border Logistics Optimization

- **Background**: A multinational logistics firm faced inefficiencies in global supply chains.

- **Solution**: Integrated telematics with predictive analytics to streamline operations.

- **Result**: Reduced delivery times by 20% and saved $50 million annually.

2. Smart City Success

- **Background**: Copenhagen aimed to become carbon-neutral by 2030.

- **Solution**: Leveraged telematics for public transit optimization and air quality monitoring.

- **Result**: Reduced emissions by 40% and improved commuter satisfaction.

3. Disaster Relief Management

- **Background**: Southeast Asia experienced devastating floods, requiring coordinated rescue efforts.

- **Solution**: Telematics tracked rescue vehicles and allocated supplies efficiently.

  Result: Accelerated relief efforts, saving thousands of lives.

9. Key Takeaways

- Telematics is driving innovation globally but faces challenges such as regulatory discrepancies, infrastructure gaps, and data privacy concerns.

- Collaboration among regions, industries, and governments is essential to harmonize standards and unlock telematics' full potential.

- Emerging trends like AI, blockchain, and quantum computing will redefine telematics systems, enabling seamless global integration.

- By addressing these challenges, telematics can play a pivotal role in achieving global sustainability goals and transforming industries worldwide.

Chapter 13 The Ethical Implications of Telematics

Introduction

Telematics has unlocked immense possibilities across industries, enabling data-driven decision-making, operational efficiency, and personalized services. However, this technological revolution also brings ethical dilemmas, particularly concerning privacy, fairness, and accountability. How organizations navigate these challenges will define telematics' long-term societal impact.

Consider this: In 2022, a global telematics provider faced public backlash after a breach exposed sensitive data from 50,000 vehicles, sparking debates on ethical responsibilities in data collection and management (Frost & Sullivan, 2023). This chapter delves into the ethical challenges of telematics and outlines strategies to address them while fostering trust and transparency.

2. Key Ethical Concerns in Telematics

1. Data Privacy and Ownership

- **Concern**: Who owns the vast amounts of data generated by telematics systems? How should it be used?

- **Real-World Example**:

    o A logistics company tracked employees' locations during off-hours, violating their privacy and facing legal challenges.

- **Proposed Solutions**:

    o Adopt transparent data-sharing policies.

- o Use blockchain to empower users with data ownership and consent mechanisms.

2. Surveillance and Autonomy

- **Concern**: Over-monitoring employees, drivers, or patients may infringe on their autonomy and create a culture of distrust.

- **Real-World Example**:

  - o Delivery drivers protested telematics systems that monitored personal habits, claiming it compromised their autonomy.

- **Proposed Solutions**:

  - o Focus on anonymized performance data rather than intrusive individual tracking.

  - o Provide users with opt-in choices for non-essential monitoring.

3. Algorithmic Bias and Fairness

- **Concern**: Biases in telematics algorithms can lead to unfair outcomes, such as higher insurance premiums for urban drivers.

- **Real-World Example**:

  - o An insurance provider used telematics data to determine premiums, unfairly penalizing urban residents due to biased traffic patterns.

- **Proposed Solutions**:

  - o Conduct regular algorithmic audits to detect and eliminate biases.

  - o Train models on diverse datasets to improve equity.

4. Regulatory Compliance

- **Concern**: Navigating varying global regulations (e.g., GDPR, CCPA) while ensuring ethical data use is complex.

- **Frameworks**: GDPR, CCPA, ISO 27001, UNECE WP.29.

- **Proposed Solutions**:

    o   Develop global compliance teams.

    o   Use encryption and advanced cybersecurity tools to meet regulatory standards.

3. Ethical Challenges in Industry Applications

1. Transportation and Logistics

- **Challenge**: Tracking employee performance may blur the line between performance metrics and personal surveillance.

- **Example**: A logistics firm monitored driver behavior excessively, causing employee dissatisfaction.

- **Solution**: Balance operational tracking with respect for personal privacy.

2. Insurance and Risk Assessment

- **Challenge**: Telematics-based insurance models risk reinforcing biases, leading to discriminatory pricing.

- **Example**: Policies disproportionately penalized urban drivers for high traffic density.

- **Solution**: Incorporate fairness metrics into insurance algorithms.

3. Healthcare and Patient Monitoring

- **Challenge**: Telematics in healthcare (e.g., wearable devices) may inadvertently reveal sensitive patient data.

- **Example**: A healthcare provider faced criticism after wearable data was used for marketing purposes without consent.

- **Solution**: Encrypt patient data and restrict its use to medical purposes only.

4. Agriculture and Environmental Data

- **Challenge**: Telematics in agriculture generates vast environmental data, raising concerns about misuse by external entities.

- **Solution**: Establish clear data-sharing agreements to protect farmers' interests.

4. Proactive Ethical Framework for Telematics

1. **Transparency**:

   o Communicate clearly what data is collected, how it is used, and who has access.

   o Example: Use user-friendly dashboards to allow individuals to review and control their data.

2. **Consent**:

   o Obtain explicit user consent before collecting or processing data.

   o Example: Provide clear opt-in options for tracking and analytics.

3. **Bias Mitigation**:

   o Conduct regular AI audits and train models on inclusive datasets.

   o Example: Ensure insurance algorithms consider diverse driving conditions.

4. **Accountability**:

- o Appoint ethics officers to oversee telematics programs and address violations proactively.

- o Example: Implement organizational policies for immediate remediation of ethical lapses.

5. **User Empowerment**:

- o Allow individuals to access, edit, or delete their data easily.

- o Example: Enable blockchain-based solutions for user-managed data access.

5. Emerging Technologies Addressing Ethics

1. Blockchain for Data Integrity and Transparency

- **Application**: Decentralized storage ensures tamper-proof records and user-controlled access.

- **Example**: Blockchain-based telematics systems allow users to grant or revoke data-sharing permissions securely.

2. Explainable AI (XAI) for Accountability

- **Application**: XAI enhances trust by making AI decision making processes transparent.

- **Example**: An insurance provider used XAI to explain premium calculations, reducing customer complaints.

3. Privacy-Enhancing Technologies (PETs)

- **Application**: Techniques like differential privacy and homomorphic encryption protect sensitive data during analysis.

- **Example**: A telematics provider anonymized data to ensure compliance with GDPR while retaining analytical insights.

6. Case Studies and Ethical Dilemmas

1. Employee Monitoring Backlash

- **Background**: A logistics company implemented telematics to monitor driver performance.

- **Dilemma**: Employees protested intrusive tracking that extended beyond work hours.

- **Solution**: Shifted to anonymized fleet-level metrics, balancing operational goals with privacy.

2. Insurance Bias in Urban Areas

- **Background**: An insurer used telematics data for risk assessment.

  Dilemma: Algorithms penalized urban drivers unfairly due to higher traffic congestion.

- **Solution**: Updated models to incorporate contextual factors, creating fairer pricing systems.

3. Data Breach in Fleet Management

- **Background**: A fleet management platform experienced a breach, exposing vehicle and driver data.

- **Dilemma**: Customers questioned the company's ability to secure sensitive information.

- **Solution**: Integrated blockchain for secure data storage and implemented regular security audits.

7. Key Takeaways

- Telematics brings significant ethical challenges, including data privacy concerns, surveillance risks, and algorithmic bias.

- Organizations must adopt frameworks emphasizing transparency, consent, and user empowerment to address these concerns.

- Emerging technologies like blockchain, explainable AI, and privacy-enhancing techniques offer viable solutions to ethical dilemmas.

- Case studies highlight the importance of balancing innovation with fairness and accountability.

- By prioritizing ethics, telematics can deliver transformative value while respecting societal values and individual rights.

Chapter 14 The Business Case for Telematics

Introduction

Telematics systems have emerged as transformative tools for businesses across industries, enabling operational efficiency, cost reduction, and enhanced customer satisfaction. By leveraging real-time data and predictive analytics, telematics drives competitive advantages, helping businesses adapt to rapidly evolving markets.

Consider this: Companies adopting telematics report a 2030% reduction in operational costs within the first year, highlighting the ROI potential of these systems (McKinsey & Company, 2023). This chapter explores how telematics delivers measurable business value while addressing challenges in adoption.

2. Telematics and Cost Reduction

Telematics systems are powerful drivers of cost savings, providing tangible benefits in several key areas:

1. Fuel Savings

- **How It Works**: Telematics monitors driver behavior, optimizes routes, and minimizes idling to reduce fuel consumption.

- **Example**: UPS saved 10 million gallons of fuel annually through telematics-powered route planning and idle-time reduction.

  Impact: Fleet operators report up to 20% savings in fuel costs after implementing telematics.

2. Maintenance Cost Optimization

- **How It Works**: Predictive analytics identify potential issues before they escalate, reducing costly unplanned repairs.

- **Example**: A logistics company reduced maintenance expenses by 30% by leveraging telematics for engine health monitoring and diagnostics.

- **Impact**: Proactive maintenance extends vehicle lifespan and reduces downtime.

3. Operational Efficiency

- **How It Works**: Automating processes like asset tracking and fleet management reduces labor-intensive manual tasks.

- **Example**: An international shipping company reduced administrative overhead by 25% by automating shipment tracking with telematics.

- **Impact**: Faster workflows and reduced operational costs.

3. Telematics and Productivity Gains

1. Driver Performance Monitoring

- **How It Works**: Telematics tracks metrics like speed, braking, and acceleration, providing feedback to drivers and fleet managers.

  Example: A delivery company improved driver safety and reduced incidents by 15% after introducing telematics-based performance reviews.

- **Impact**: Enhanced driver safety and productivity.

2. Streamlined Workflows

- **How It Works**: Telematics integrates with business systems, enabling real-time tracking and automated scheduling.

- **Example**: A courier service cut delivery times by 25% through automated dispatching and live fleet updates.

- **Impact**: Improved delivery efficiency and reduced manual interventions.

4. Customer Satisfaction and Market Differentiation

1. Real-Time Updates and Transparency

- **How It Works**: Telematics enables real-time tracking and delivery notifications, improving customer trust and satisfaction.

- **Example**: An e-commerce giant improved customer retention by 15% after integrating telematics for accurate delivery updates.

- **Impact**: Enhanced customer experience and loyalty.

2. Sustainability and Brand Image

How It Works: Telematics supports eco-friendly practices like route optimization and emissions monitoring, boosting brand reputation.

- **Example**: An EV fleet company gained market share by marketing its telematics-driven sustainability efforts.

- **Impact**: Competitive advantage through environmental responsibility.

5. Challenges of Telematics Implementation

1. Upfront Costs

- **Challenge**: Initial investments in hardware, software, and training deter smaller businesses.

- **Solution**: Use scalable cloud-based solutions with pay-asyou-go pricing to reduce financial barriers.

2. Integration Complexity

- **Challenge**: Legacy systems may not seamlessly integrate with modern telematics platforms.

- **Solution**: Middleware and standardized APIs simplify integration processes.

3. Workforce Resistance

- **Challenge**: Employees may resist telematics adoption due to concerns about surveillance or unfamiliarity with the technology.

- **Solution**: Conduct training sessions and emphasize telematics' benefits for safety and productivity.

6. ROI Metrics for Telematics

Measuring the return on investment (ROI) for telematics involves tracking key performance indicators:

1. Fuel Efficiency

- Metric: Percentage reduction in fuel costs per vehicle.

- Example: A trucking company saved $5 million annually through telematics-driven fuel optimization.

2. Maintenance Savings

- Metric: Decrease in unplanned repairs or breakdowns.

- Example: Fleet managers reduced maintenance costs by 30% using predictive maintenance tools.

3. Delivery Performance Improvements

- Metric: Increase in on-time deliveries and reduction in delays.

- Example: A logistics provider improved delivery punctuality by 20% after implementing telematics-based route planning.

4. Customer Retention

- Metric: Percentage increase in repeat business due to enhanced service quality.

- Example: Retailers reported a 10% rise in customer loyalty after integrating real-time delivery notifications.

7. Case Studies and Real-World Examples

1. Fleet Optimization

- **Background**: A logistics firm faced high fuel costs and inefficiencies in route planning.

- **Solution**: Introduced telematics for real-time fleet tracking and route optimization.

- **Result**: Achieved 20% fuel savings and 30% improvement in delivery times.

2. E-Commerce Delivery Excellence

- **Background**: An online retailer faced complaints about late deliveries and lack of tracking.

- **Solution**: Integrated telematics for real-time delivery updates and dynamic routing.

- **Result**: Improved customer satisfaction by 15% and reduced complaints by 40%.

3. Predictive Maintenance in Public Transport

- **Background**: A city's bus fleet experienced frequent breakdowns, disrupting schedules.

- **Solution**: Implemented telematics to monitor engine health and predict maintenance needs.

- **Result**: Reduced breakdowns by 35%, enhancing reliability and public satisfaction.

8. Key Takeaways

- Telematics delivers measurable business benefits through cost reduction, productivity gains, and improved customer satisfaction.

- ROI metrics like fuel savings, maintenance cost reductions, and customer retention highlight its tangible value.

- Challenges such as upfront costs and integration complexity can be addressed with scalable solutions, middleware tools, and employee training programs.

- Businesses adopting telematics gain a competitive edge, positioning themselves as leaders in innovation, efficiency, and sustainability.

Chapter 15 Telematics and the Road Ahead

Introduction

Telematics is on the brink of a new frontier, poised to transform industries, cities, and global operations. From enabling real-time communication across devices to driving sustainability goals, telematics is shaping the future of connectivity and innovation.

Consider this: By 2040, telematics is expected to power 90% of global smart city operations, revolutionizing transportation, energy, and public services (Allied Market Research, 2023). This chapter explores the opportunities, challenges, and transformative potential of telematics as we move toward a hyperconnected world.

2. Hyperconnected Ecosystems

Vehicles, Infrastructure, and IoT Integration

- Vision: Telematics will create a seamless ecosystem where vehicles, infrastructure, and IoT devices communicate in real time.

- Example: In Singapore, telematics-powered traffic management systems synchronize traffic lights, reducing congestion by 25%.

- Future Impact:

    o Improve urban mobility and enhance road safety.

    o Reduce commute times and fuel consumption.

Smart Cities and Telematics

- Vision: Telematics will serve as the backbone for smart cities, integrating public transportation, energy grids, and environmental monitoring.

- Example: Copenhagen uses telematics to optimize public transport schedules and monitor air quality, achieving a 40% reduction in emissions.

- Future Impact:

  o Enhance quality of life and drive eco-friendly urban development.

3. Digital Twins and Predictive Modeling

Real-Time Simulations for Optimization

- Vision: Digital twins will create virtual replicas of physical systems, such as cities or logistics networks, for real-time optimization.

- Example: A logistics company uses digital twins to simulate delivery routes, improving efficiency by 30%.

- Future Impact:

  o Enable dynamic decision-making and proactive problem-solving.

Disaster Preparedness and Infrastructure Planning

- Vision: Digital twins will help cities prepare for natural disasters by simulating scenarios and optimizing resource allocation.

  Example: A city government uses telematics and digital twins to coordinate flood responses, reducing recovery time by 50%.

- Future Impact:
  - o Save lives and minimize economic losses during emergencies.

4. Sustainability and Telematics

Enabling Net-Zero Emissions

- Vision: Telematics systems will play a pivotal role in reducing emissions through optimized routes, EV integration, and renewable energy adoption.

- Example: An EV fleet operator reduced emissions by 30% using telematics to optimize charging schedules.

- Future Impact:
  - o Accelerate progress toward global sustainability goals.

Resource Conservation and Renewable Energy

- Vision: Telematics will integrate with renewable energy grids to balance supply and demand dynamically.

- Example: Renewable energy providers use telematics to predict energy surpluses and redirect them to high-demand areas.

- Future Impact:
  - o Maximize energy efficiency and reduce waste.

5. Quantum Computing and Advanced Analytics

Logistics Optimization

- Vision: Quantum computing wil solve complex optimization problems in seconds, transforming logistics and supply chains.

- Example: A multinational retailer uses quantum algorithms to manage inventory across thousands of locations, reducing costs by 20%.

- Future Impact:

    o Enable real-time decision-making for global operations.

Revolutionizing Complex Systems

- Vision: Quantum computing will revolutionize telematics by processing vast datasets from IoT devices and autonomous vehicles.

- Example: Autonomous fleets use quantum-powered telematics to optimize city-wide navigation and reduce congestion.

- Future Impact:

    o Drive innovation in transportation, healthcare, and energy.

6. Personalized Mobility and Services

Dynamic Ride-Sharing Solutions

Vision: Telematics will enable dynamic, on-demand transportation services, adapting to user needs in real time.

- Example: Ride-sharing apps use telematics to pool passengers with similar destinations, reducing travel costs and emissions. Future Impact:

    o Enhance accessibility and convenience for urban commuters.

User-Centric Innovations

- Vision: Telematics will deliver hyper-personalized experiences, from route preferences to autonomous delivery systems.

- Example: Autonomous taxis equipped with telematics adjust routes based on passenger preferences and real-time traffic data.

- Future Impact:

    o Transform customer experiences and create new business opportunities.

7. Global Collaboration for Telematics Adoption

Data Sharing Across Borders

- Vision: Shared telematics data will optimize global logistics and urban mobility.

    Example: Logistics companies in Europe and Asia collaborate to streamline cross-border transportation using shared telematics insights.

- Future Impact:

    o   Foster international efficiency and innovation.

Standardization and Interoperability

- Vision: Unified frameworks will ensure seamless telematics integration worldwide.

- Example: Global adoption of UNECE WP.29 cybersecurity standards ensures secure telematics operations.

- Future Impact:

o   Simplify deployment and enhance system reliability.

8. Future Opportunities Across Industries

Healthcare

- Vision: Telematics will enable remote patient monitoring and predictive diagnostics.

- Example: Wearables transmit real-time health data to doctors, improving patient outcomes.

- Future Impact:

    o   Transform healthcare delivery and reduce costs.

Agriculture

- Vision: Precision farming will use telematics-powered IoT sensors to optimize soil, water, and crop management.

    Example: Farmers use telematics to reduce water usage by 30% while increasing yields by 20%.

- Future Impact: o Ensure food security and resource efficiency.

    ### Retail and Logistics

- Vision: Telematics will streamline supply chains, improving inventory management and delivery timelines.

- Example: Retailers use real-time telematics data to prevent stockouts and reduce delivery delays.

- Future Impact:

    o   Enhance customer satisfaction and operational efficiency.

9. Addressing Challenges in Telematics

Technological Barriers

- Challenge: Scaling IoT infrastructure for billions of connected devices.

- Solution: Invest in 5G networks and edge computing to enhance scalability.

Regulatory and Ethical Concerns

- Challenge: Navigating global regulations and ensuring ethical use of telematics data.

- Solution: Standardize policies and adopt transparencyfocused practices.

Workforce Readiness

- Challenge: Preparing employees for telematics-based operations.

- Solution: Develop comprehensive training programs and certifications.

10. Key Takeaways

- Telematics is poised to revolutionize industries and societies, enabling hyperconnected ecosystems, digital twins, and sustainable operations.

- Addressing challenges like technological scalability, regulatory compliance, and workforce readiness is essential for widespread adoption.

- Emerging technologies like quantum computing and AI will redefine telematics' capabilities, driving innovation and global efficiency.

- Collaboration among governments, businesses, and organizations will ensure telematics delivers on its promise to create a smarter, more connected world.

Chapter 16 Conclusion and Final Thoughts on Telematics

Introduction

Telematics has emerged as a transformative technology, reshaping industries, improving lives, and paving the way for a smarter, more connected world. Its integration with technologies like AI, blockchain, and IoT has unlocked possibilities once confined to science fiction.

Consider this: By 2040, telematics is expected to save businesses over $500 billion annually through operational efficiency and resource optimization, while simultaneously contributing to global sustainability goals (Frost & Sullivan, 2023). As we close this exploration of telematics, let us reflect on its journey, its current role, and its future potential to address the challenges of tomorrow.

2. Recap of Key Themes

1. Technological Transformation

- Telematics has revolutionized industries by enabling realtime connectivity, predictive analytics, and autonomous systems.

- **Example**: In transportation, telematics powers autonomous vehicles, ensuring safer and more efficient roads.

- **Impact**: From logistics to healthcare, telematics fosters innovation, drives operational excellence, and improves decision-making.

2. Economic and Operational Impact

- Telematics drives significant cost savings, boosts productivity, and enhances customer satisfaction.

- **Example**: Businesses report a 20-30% reduction in operational expenses within the first year of adopting telematics (McKinsey & Company, 2021).

- **Impact**: By reducing inefficiencies and enhancing resource utilization, telematics offers unparalleled ROI.

3. Sustainability Contributions

- Telematics is a cornerstone of global sustainability efforts, enabling resource conservation, emissions reduction, and eco-friendly urban planning.

- **Example**: EV fleets leveraging telematics have reduced emissions by 30%, accelerating progress toward net-zero goals.

- **Impact**: Through smarter systems, telematics supports global initiatives like the Paris Agreement and the UN's Sustainable Development Goals (SDGs).

4. Ethical and Regulatory Considerations

- The integration of telematics has raised critical ethical questions, including data privacy, algorithmic fairness, and regulatory compliance.

- **Example**: Compliance with GDPR and CCPA ensures that telematics systems prioritize transparency and user trust.

- **Impact**: Ethical and regulatory adherence is key to sustainable adoption and public confidence in telematics.

3. Vision for the Future

1. Global Collaboration and Unified Standards

- **Vision**: Foster international partnerships to harmonize telematics regulations and create interoperable systems.

- **Example**: Multinational logistics companies share telematics data to optimize global supply chains, reducing delays and emissions.

- **Future Impact**: Unified standards will accelerate innovation, simplify deployments, and ensure seamless global operations.

2. Addressing Societal Challenges ⬚ Urban Congestion:

  o Telematics can optimize traffic flow, reducing urban congestion and improving mobility.

  o **Example**: Smart cities integrate telematics to synchronize traffic lights, cutting commute times by 25%.

- **Climate Resilience**:

  o Predictive models powered by telematics enhance disaster preparedness and resource allocation.

  o **Example**: During floods, telematics systems track rescue vehicles, ensuring timely relief efforts.

- **Equitable Technology Access**:

  o Telematics can bridge the digital divide by making advanced technologies accessible to underserved regions.

3. Emerging Technologies and Integration Quantum Computing:

  o Solve complex logistics and operational challenges at unprecedented speeds.

  o **Example**: Quantum-powered telematics enables dynamic fleet management during global disruptions.

- **AI and Explainable Analytics**:
  - o Enhance predictive capabilities while ensuring transparency in decision-making processes.
  - o **Example**: AI-driven telematics systems predict engine failures, reducing downtime by 25%.
- **Digital Twins**:
  - o Virtual replicas of physical systems optimize realtime decision-making and long-term planning.
  - o **Example**: Cities use digital twins to simulate traffic patterns and design efficient infrastructure.

4. Acknowledgment of Challenges

1. Data Privacy and Ethical Concerns

- **Challenge**: Ensuring data is collected and used responsibly while safeguarding individual privacy.
- **Solution**: Adopt user-centric data controls and comply with global privacy regulations.

2. Infrastructure and Cost Barriers

- **Challenge**: Scaling telematics infrastructure in developing regions and cost-sensitive industries.
- **Solution**: Leverage cloud-based solutions, public-private partnerships, and scalable IoT technologies.

3. Workforce Readiness

- **Challenge**: Preparing employees for telematics-enabled workflows and operations.

- **Solution**: Invest in training programs, certifications, and upskilling initiatives to build a future-ready workforce.

5. Inspirational Closing

As we stand on the brink of a hyperconnected future, telematics is more than a technology—it is a catalyst for change. It empowers industries to innovate, governments to plan smarter cities, and societies to embrace sustainability. The path forward will not be without challenges, but with collaboration, ethical practices, and technological advancements, telematics can create a future where efficiency, equity, and environmental stewardship converge.

Closing Thought:

"Telematics is not just shaping industries; it is shaping the world. Its transformative potential lies in our collective ability to innovate responsibly and inclusively. Together, we can build a future where connectivity drives progress and technology serves humanity."

6. Key Takeaways

- Telematics has revolutionized industries through real-time connectivity, predictive analytics, and operational efficiency.

- It is a driving force for sustainability, enabling emissions reduction, resource conservation, and eco-friendly innovations.

- Challenges like data privacy, infrastructure costs, and workforce readiness must be addressed for widespread adoption.

- Collaboration among stakeholders is crucial to harmonizing standards, fostering innovation, and realizing telematics' full potential.

- The future of telematics is bright, offering endless possibilities for industries, societies, and the planet.

Appendices

Appendix A: Glossary of Telematics Terms

A comprehensive list of essential telematics terms and their definitions for readers to reference.

- **Telematics**: The integration of telecommunications and informatics to enable real-time data collection, transmission, and analysis.

- **V2X Communication**: Vehicle-to-everything communication that allows vehicles to interact with infrastructure, other vehicles, and pedestrians.

- **Digital Twin**: A virtual model of a physical system used for real-time monitoring and decision-making.

- **GDPR**: General Data Protection Regulation, a European law ensuring data privacy and protection.

Appendix B: Key Telematics Technologies

An overview of the core technologies driving telematics innovation.

1. **5G Connectivity**:

   o Enables ultra-low latency and high-speed data transmission for real-time telematics.

2. **Artificial Intelligence (AI)**:

   o Powers predictive analytics, route optimization, and adaptive systems.

3. **Blockchain**:

Provides secure, transparent data-sharing frameworks to enhance trust.

4. **Internet of Things (IoT)**:

   o Sensors and connected devices that gather and transmit actionable data.

Appendix C: Global Standards and Regulations

A guide to international standards and regulatory frameworks shaping telematics adoption.

1. **GDPR** (European Union):

   o Governs data protection and privacy, ensuring transparency and accountability.

2. **ISO 27001**:

   o Sets standards for information security management systems.

3. **UNECE WP.29**:

   o Cybersecurity regulations for connected vehicles to ensure data integrity.

4. **FMCSA ELD Mandates** (North America):

   o Requires electronic logging devices in commercial fleets to improve safety and compliance.

Appendix D: Tools and Resources for Telematics Adoption

A curated list of tools, platforms, and resources for businesses and individuals implementing telematics.

Platforms:

- **Geotab**: Fleet management and telematics solutions.
- **Verizon Connect**: Comprehensive telematics and workforce management tools.
- **Samsara**: Real-time fleet tracking and operational insights.

  Resources:

- **Case Studies**: McKinsey's *Transforming Logistics with Telematics.*
- **Courses**: Coursera's *Telematics and IoT Fundamentals.*

Appendix E: Industry-Specific Applications of Telematics

A breakdown of telematics use cases across major industries.

1. **Transportation and Logistics**:

   o Route optimization, fleet tracking, and fuel monitoring.

2. **Healthcare**:

   o Remote patient monitoring and emergency response coordination.

3. **Agriculture**:

   Precision farming with IoT-enabled soil and crop monitoring.

4. **Retail and Supply Chain**:

   o Real-time inventory tracking and predictive delivery analytics.

Appendix F: ROI Calculation Framework

A practical guide for calculating the return on investment (ROI) for telematics systems.

1. **Initial Costs**:

    o   Hardware, software, training, and integration expenses.

2. **Operational Savings**:

    o   Fuel efficiency, reduced maintenance, and labor savings.

3. **Productivity Gains**:

    o   Enhanced workflows and reduced downtime.

4. **Formula**:

    o   ROI = [(Savings + Gains - Costs) / Costs] × 100%

Appendix G: Case Studies and Success Stories

Real-world examples showcasing telematics' impact across industries.

1. **UPS**:

    Saved 10 million gallons of fuel annually through route optimization. 2. **Copenhagen Smart City**:

    o   Reduced emissions by 40% using telematics-driven urban planning.

3. **Fleet Management Company**:

    o   Improved on-time deliveries by 20% with predictive analytics.

Appendix H: Emerging Trends in Telematics

Highlighting trends shaping the future of telematics.

1. **Quantum Computing**:

    o Revolutionizing logistics with real-time optimization.

2. **Digital Twins**:

    o Creating virtual replicas for smarter decision making.

3. **Personalized Mobility**:

    o Enabling user-centric transportation solutions like autonomous ride-sharing.

Appendix I: Ethical Guidelines for Telematics

A framework to ensure ethical telematics implementation.

1. **Transparency**:

    Clearly communicate data collection and usage policies.

2. **User Empowerment**: o Allow users to access, modify, or delete their data.

3. **Bias Mitigation**:

    o Conduct regular audits to ensure fairness in AIdriven systems.

Appendix J: Frequently Asked Questions (FAQs)

Answers to common questions about telematics.

1. What is telematics, and why is it important?

Telematics integrates telecommunications and informatics to enable real-time data collection, analysis, and sharing. It is important because it:

- Optimizes operational efficiency.
- Enhances safety and decision-making.
- Drives innovation in industries like transportation, healthcare, and logistics.

2. **How does telematics benefit businesses?**

Telematics provides businesses with:

- **Cost Savings**: Reduces fuel consumption, maintenance expenses, and operational inefficiencies.

- **Productivity Gains**: Streamlines workflows through automation and real-time tracking.

- **Customer Satisfaction**: Improves service quality with accurate delivery updates and transparent operations.

- **Sustainability**: Reduces emissions and supports ecofriendly practices.

3. **What challenges exist in adopting telematics systems?**

Common challenges include:

- **Upfront Costs**: Initial investment in hardware, software, and training.

- **Integration Complexity**: Compatibility issues with legacy systems.

- **Data Privacy Concerns**: Ensuring compliance with regulations like GDPR and CCPA.

- **Workforce Resistance**: Overcoming skepticism or unfamiliarity among employees.

4. **How is telematics data protected and secured?**

Telematics data is safeguarded through:

- **Encryption**: Ensuring data is secure during transmission and storage.

- **Blockchain**: Providing tamper-proof, decentralized datasharing mechanisms.

- **Regulatory Compliance**: Adhering to global standards like GDPR and ISO 27001.

- **Access Controls**: Limiting data access to authorized users only.

5. **What industries benefit the most from telematics?**

Industries leveraging telematics include:

1. **Transportation and Logistics**: Fleet management, route optimization, and fuel monitoring.

2. **Healthcare**: Remote patient monitoring and emergency response systems.

3. **Agriculture**: Precision farming and irrigation management.

4. **Retail and Supply Chain**: Real-time inventory tracking and delivery optimization.

6. **How does telematics support sustainability?**

Telematics contributes to sustainability by:

- Reducing emissions through route optimization and idletime reduction.

- Supporting renewable energy adoption with dynamic grid management.

- Promoting eco-friendly practices in smart cities and logistics.

7. **Can small businesses afford telematics systems?**

Yes. Modern telematics solutions offer scalable, cloud-based options with pay-as-you-go pricing, making them accessible to businesses of all sizes.

8. **How is telematics evolving with emerging technologies?**

Telematics is integrating with:

- **AI and Machine Learning**: Enabling predictive analytics and dynamic decision-making.

- **5G Connectivity**: Supporting real-time communication and low-latency applications.

- **Quantum Computing**: Revolutionizing logistics optimization and data processing.

- **Digital Twins**: Providing virtual simulations for better planning and management.

9. **What ethical considerations are involved in telematics?**

Ethical concerns include:

- **Data Privacy**: Ensuring individuals have control over their data.

- **Algorithmic Bias**: Preventing discrimination in AI-driven systems.

- **Surveillance and Autonomy**: Balancing monitoring with employee and user rights.

10. What are the key trends shaping telematics' future?

Key trends include:

- Expansion of IoT ecosystems connecting billions of devices.

- Increased adoption of autonomous vehicles and personalized mobility solutions.

- Greater focus on sustainability and resource conservation.

- Integration of telematics with smart cities and global logistics networks.

Appendix K: Further Reading and References

A list of books, articles, and research papers for further exploration.

Books:

- *The Connected World: Understanding Telematics and IoT* by A. Smith.

Articles:

- McKinsey & Company: *The Future of Telematics Innovation*.

Research Papers:

- OECD: *Standards and Regulations for Telematics Integration*.

Appendix L: Glossary of Acronyms

A quick reference for commonly used acronyms in telematics.

- **IoT**: Internet of Things

- **V2X**: Vehicle-to-Everything Communication

- **ELD**: Electronic Logging Device

- **GDPR**: General Data Protection Regulation

References

General Telematics

- Allied Market Research. (2023). *The future of telematics: Trends shaping industries.* Retrieved from https://www.alliedmarketresearch.com

- Frost & Sullivan. (2023). *Telematics and the road ahead: A global perspective.* Retrieved from https://www.frost.com

- McKinsey & Company. (2021). *Driving efficiency and sustainability with telematics.* Retrieved from https://www.mckinsey.com **Technological Advancements**

- International Transport Forum. (2022). Emerging technologies in telematics: AI, blockchain, and IoT. OECD Publishing. Retrieved from https://www.oecd.org

- PwC. (2023). How 5G and IoT are transforming telematics. Retrieved from https://www.pwc.com

- IBM Research. (2022). Blockchain and its role in secure telematics ecosystems. Retrieved from https://www.ibm.com

Applications Across Industries

- Harvard Business Review. (2023). Telematics in healthcare: The rise of connected systems. Retrieved from https://hbr.org

John Deere. (2022). Precision agriculture: How telematics is revolutionizing farming. Retrieved from https://www.deere.com

- UPS Case Study. (2023). Saving fuel through route optimization with telematics. Retrieved from https://www.ups.com **Cybersecurity and Privacy**

- NIST. (2023). Cybersecurity standards for connected vehicles. Retrieved from https://www.nist.gov

- GDPR Compliance Guide. (2023). Ensuring privacy in telematics data usage. Retrieved from https://gdpr-info.eu

- Symantec. (2022). Cybersecurity in IoT-driven telematics systems. Retrieved from https://www.symantec.com

Sustainability and Environmental Impact

- World Economic Forum. (2023). Telematics and sustainability: Enabling net-zero emissions. Retrieved from https://www.weforum.org

- UNEP. (2022). Smart cities and the role of telematics in environmental monitoring. Retrieved from https://www.unep.org

- Tesla Case Study. (2023). Leveraging telematics for EV fleet efficiency. Retrieved from https://www.tesla.com

Global Collaboration and Standards

- UNECE. (2023). WP.29 Cybersecurity regulations for connected vehicles. Retrieved from https://unece.org

- ISO. (2022) Telematicsand information security: ISO 27001 implementation. Retrieved from https://www.iso.org

- ITU. (2023). Global standards for telematics in smart cities. Retrieved from https://www.itu.int **Future Trends**

- Deloitte Insights. (2023). Digital twins and the future of telematics. Retrieved from https://www2.deloitte.com

- Gartner. (2023). Emerging trends in telematics: Quantum computing and AI. Retrieved from https://www.gartner.com

- Accenture Research. (2022). Hyperconnected ecosystems: Telematics at the forefront of innovation. Retrieved from https://www.accenture.com **Ethical Considerations**

- IEEE. (2023). Ethical frameworks for telematics and AI systems. Retrieved from https://www.ieee.org

- Harvard Kennedy School. (2022). Algorithmic bias in telematics: Ensuring fairness in predictive analytics. Retrieved from https://www.hks.harvard.edu

- Privacy International. (2023). Balancing innovation and privacy in telematics adoption. Retrieved from https://privacyinternational.org

Business Impacts and ROI

- Forrester Research. (2023). Calculating ROI for telematics systems. Retrieved from https://go.forrester.com

  Gartner. (2022). Telematics adoption: Cost-saving opportunities for businesses. Retrieved from https://www.gartner.com

- Bain & Company. (2023). How businesses leverage telematics for market differentiation. Retrieved from https://www.bain.com